MEETINGS IN HIS KINGDOM

Jesus Personally Leading His Church . . .

In Home, City, and Multi-City Gatherings

As always, if we can help you in any way,
please contact the church here at:
P.O. Box 68309, Indianapolis, Indiana 46268

ISBN 0-9627202-0-8

Meetings in His Kingdom

Table of Contents

PART 2: The Large Family . . . the City Church

PART 3: Multi-City Gatherings

Meetings in His Kingdom

Jesus Personally Leading His Church . . . In Home, City, and Multi-City Gatherings

Introduction

The following was first taught verbally (originating from notes scratched on a McDonald's napkin) in a living room in the Midwest in 1986. It was spoken to a group of believers that is neither protestant nor catholic, neither charismatic, pentecostal, fundamental, or evangelical – in the typical sense that those labels are used. As you read you'll notice many direct excerpts from that evening. Such excerpts throughout this book may sound "personal" (or colloquially awkward and redundant) for that reason. Frankly, I don't even want to take the time to pretty anything up – there's too much work to do. The thoughts contained here are nothing more than just one weak, sometimes-failing-but-determined brother opening his heart to his friends. The subject? God's People cultivating a deep relationship with their God and one another. It's about gathering "in His Name" – letting Jesus, our Lord, have His way utterly in our midst.

Two or three thoughts to help you along the way as you read: Much of what is contained in these pages is not simply the exposition of Scripture, but the **application** of

Scriptural Truths. The focus will be, as Paul's often was, on the nature of practical Life, walking with Jesus Christ in His Kingdom. Later on in the book, in the last two sections especially, you'll discover more in the "Vision" realm than the practical thoughts that permeate the early chapters. Hang tough! Also, several have suggested that the footnotes may be amongst the most important parts of this book. Please take the time to read them, to gain the most from the investment you'll make in digging in to all of this.

You will find, I hope, that this writing is not about a "new way to have church." Those of us who worked together to offer these thoughts to you are in total agreement: We want nothing whatsoever to do with being known as "those folks that talk about meetings." YUK! Our hearts, and I believe our way of Life, is about JESUS, not meetings. This writing is about HIM, and something nearly foreign to western, twentieth-century thinking: It is about a Kingdom.[1]

Few in a democratic society can even fathom the true meaning and administration of a "Kingdom." Just as an example of our culture's arrogance and disloyalties, masses applaud the insulting two-hour television rebuttals to the President's "State of the Union Address." How can we understand a "Kingdom" when we are so committed to "every man doing what is right in his own eyes?" ("Submission" is never submission – if we must agree first.)

In spite of the vocabulary used during "worship time," most of christendom today is pretty far from being, really, an expression of the Kingdom of God. Absolute loyalty, and prostrate unquestioning obedience and devotion, are mostly passe in our "modern" world. (Neat worship hours are still "in," however.) Dare we truly penetrate the meaning of the present manifestation of His Lordship "in our midst?" As Paul said, "Now!"[2] *(And I certainly am not speaking of a "social utopia." I am speaking of the same Glory manifested in a*

---

[1] Isaiah 9:6-7; 2Cor.3:17-18; Acts 3:17-23; Mat.4:23; Lk.10:9, Acts 8:12, 28:31.

[2] Ephesians 3:10; Matthew 16:18.

*weak, but awe-some "no beauty or majesty" People that was
manifested first in our Lord as He walked with us in the flesh.)* [3]

*To put it yet another way, this writing is about Life,
Together, as a Family, under our Father. He meant for us to
journey Together. "We being many, are one body." The poems
and song lyrics that you'll discover as you journey through
these pages are representative, I think, of this Truth. Each was
written by a member of the Body of Christ in this locale, and
offered at different times, during gatherings, and from house
to house. These offerings too, were never meant to impress
anyone but Jesus, and are simply the heart-felt expressions of
the day-to-day life of God's lambs living for Jesus and for one
another.*

*Enough said. Please feel free to "join us" in that room
that evening. More importantly, join us in the Life of liberty
meant for His Church throughout the world!* [4]

---

[3] 2Corinthians 13:4, 12:9-10; 1Corinthians 3:18, 4:10-13, 1:18-31; Isaiah
53:1-4,10.

[4] Early on I'd like to say this: We, as a part of Christ's Church in the city in
which we live, do not make any claims for ourselves. We only want to boast in our
Lord, Jesus. To point anyone towards us, rather than towards our Brother and King
and the Truth of His Word, would be a tragedy. As soon as anyone promotes
themselves, or offers themselves as a model of God's Truth (though such models are
a valid possibility if GOD does the promotion by His Grace – 1Thes.1:7, 1:6, 2:10, 14),
a fall is near. When they offer themselves as a "fishbowl" for others to look at, they
become driven by their need to protect their reputation and to promote their
paradigm. Frankly, by the time you read this book, the entire Church here – men,
women, and children – may have been sent out to other cities and countries, never
again to meet together as a whole. [That "sending" – whether via the means of
Acts 13 or Acts 8 – is always a possibility for "children of Abraham" (Heb.11:8-10,
Rom.4:16). We're not aware of any such plans God may have for us at this instant,
but we all want to have our roots, our center of gravity, in Heaven (Eph.2:6;
Col.3:1-4; Heb.11:13-16; 1Pet.2:9-12) so that we will be immediately available to God.]
My point is this: **Let the Truth of the Word of God and the Life of Jesus** be
the Standard that drives you to a healthy dissatisfaction for any environment you are
in that does not fully express God's Heart. Don't follow men or movements, but
rather let God Himself build a deep, deep conviction of His Desire for His People in
your soul. Then you will be impassioned all the days of your life for Him and His
Purposes – no matter what anyone anywhere does, or does not do. Jesus will never
disappoint you. Live, and be willing to die, for HIM.

For clarity's sake I should say again that many of the thoughts here were originally spoken directly to a church that was already living in very much the reality of "daily in public and from house to house."⁵ For that reason, if you are living in a more typical modern-day church environment, you may be a step or two out of an ability to visualize, or live in, some of what follows. At least for now. If this turns out to be the case, try to understand as much as you can, and pray that God will give increase to these Seeds in your future. But don't ever be complacent and accept less than what Jesus deserves in His People! Be a catalyst for Godly change!

This teaching was, at the time it was originally spoken, a direct challenge to some of the carnality of those early days in the local church where God had placed us. Still, there has been a continual paradox – a paradox that seems very much like that of Isaiah 53. In spite of the suffering, there has been much to be thankful for. This excerpt (from another writing) was written to describe some of what God has done in His People, His Bride, here and around the world, in spite of her weaknesses:

Jesus' Bride, His Church. She's a special Lady, a "Bride PREPARED for the return of the Groom," the King of Glory. She's "a glorious church, not having spot or wrinkle or any such thing, but holy and without blemish." She is an equal yoke for Jesus – compassionate, yet filled with fury towards hypocrisy; sensitive, yet relentlessly pursuing the completion of Her Father's business. This is the church that Jesus bought with His very Blood...

She's a church that is not bound by time and place, but visibly expresses herself "daily in public and from house to house." She's "joined and knit together by every supporting ligament," "everyone members of one-another," "confessing sins one to another," "admonishing one another daily so that none are hardened by the deceit-

---

⁵ The phrase "temple courts" referred to in Acts 2 – Acts 8, and interpreted hereafter as "in public," does not, in the Scriptures, refer to a "church building." The phrase "temple courts" in the Scriptures refers to an area that the people of Jerusalem used as a **city park**, not a religious structure erected for "services."

fulness of sin," always loving and serving and "bearing one-another's burdens" in joy and thanksgiving (and, occasionally, with a few tears). She is a "city set on a hill that cannot be hidden." Her corporate gatherings are only the overflow of what is happening on the streets and in the homes of all of her people.

"Now the multitude of those who believed were of one heart and one soul; neither did anyone say that any of the things he possessed was his own."

She's characterized by "mega power" and "mega grace." Sin is exposed and eradicated with "ever-increasing Glory" in the lives of those in the church. Captives have been, at long last, set FREE. (With more to come, by His Grace!) The singing of songs to our God isn't directed by a menu printed a week in advance, but (hopefully!) flows out of what God is doing in our midst each moment.

Together, with intimacy of relationships, we'll continue to learn to LIVE as our Lord did. Jesus, the Christ of God, now lives within us, individually and as a People - (Col. 1:26-27, 3:4; Gal.2:20; Acts 17:28; Eph.3:10, 5:18; 1Jn.2:6; Rom.8:9).[6]

The Church here has had good days and bad days (if not good months and bad months) and is readily able to admit that she still has much to learn. And at the time of this admonition (the oral teaching about meetings in His Kingdom) "way back when" . . . the baby stuff almost seemed to bury us at times. And it certainly took a lot of the fun out of gatherings or evenings when we had to deal with that baby stuff. Has it been worth it? It has been awesome. No complaints. Many tears and late nights, and much perspiration by His Priesthood over the years, but no complaints. We wouldn't go back in time for a jillion dollars.

---

[6] The Traditions of Men, P.O. Box 68230, Indianapolis, IN. 46268.

Again, you'll need to remember that this teaching came to the surface during a gathering of a church that was already walking (though childishly much of the time!) as a Priesthood of Believers. There were (and are) no "Bible Studies" – but **much** Bible. There were (and are) no "services" – but very frequent gatherings of the entire church. There were (and are) no "Prayer Meetings" – but much prayer together and separately. There were (and are) no clergymen – but there are Saints leading the way who are washed in His Blood and Enveloped by His Spirit. Frail as we are, that is at least our direction by the Grace of God, and many of the following exhortations are directly to those who have already moved (a short distance) down that Path towards letting Jesus have His Church back. As you'll be able to tell, we wrestled with it and fumbled around some, as will all who desire to get up out of the chair and test their legs! Come along with us. Jesus is fun to be around!

Chapter One

Motivation For Risk

A RE we all, I wonder, thoroughly convinced of the extreme need of our day? I read a study, only two hours before writing this page, that ought to guarantee that church-going parents are shocked into radical action in their churches. A full 75% of the young teenagers from across the country who are *part of churches*, "admit to such [sexual] practices as ___, ___, and ___."[7] (I don't want to even mention them here.) Even nearly one out of every ten *12-year-olds* in the churches have lost their virginity. Only God Himself knows how much is happening that the children in the "teen groups" and "young professionals' groups" *won't* admit. Have we learned yet that the answers don't lie in a "better youth program" or even "more Bible Studies on morality"? It is very clear that no matter how great the "worship time" is and no matter how articulate and challenging the sermons are, the statistics are the *same*. Frightening!

There *are* answers – in a real honest-to-goodness Light-Walking Church that "the gates of Hell cannot prevail against!" That doesn't describe very many churches . . . yet![8]

---

[7] Shattering the Silence: Telling the Church the Truth About Their Kids and Sexuality, Lewis, Dodd, and Tippens, Christian Communications, 1990.

[8] A man of significant insight and considerable name-recognition recently exclaimed to a large gathering of God's People that the last days would see at least two major changes in the Church:

The prime motivation for writing this book is that, in spite of what many preachers have told their congregations, there *are* real answers available to the disastrous spiritual decline of the last two thousand years. Men and women who care about the systematic destruction of their children and families and churches by the world and the prince of the world system . . . needn't give up hope. This book is not about innovation. It's about Life and death.

Admittedly, the thoughts contained in this writing are as different, for many of the same reasons, as Luther's were to the world in which he lived. No matter how true and necessary from God's vantage point the things that Luther said may have been, there were still fourteen hundred years of momentum against him. Then, as in many cases now, Clergy's appetite for control of the masses, and the general complacency of too many ("for my People love it to be so"), have resulted (and do result) in "a police state of religious look-alikes." This has intimidated and robbed God's Lambs in ways indescribably tragic. Yet not *everyone* is satisfied with the status quo. This writing is for those who want desperately to find real solutions, not just another dramatic or critical assessment of the problems that we face.

It has seemed to me, as I've cried out to the Father for understanding, that our failures are often-times not necessary. God wants to build local churches where He might manifest His Presence and delivering Power. He desires to have a corporate "habitation" for His Presence. He desires a Pillar and Foundation – a church that is walking in Light Together. He wants a body to carry and distribute the Life of His Son, poured out on flesh. He still wants to build a

---

One, that the world would grow to have a totally different opinion of the Church . . . one of respect and awe, rather than indifference or mockery.

Second (and very much related to the first in my estimation), that Christianity itself would be expressed in ways that are totally different from today's expression. Amen. A description of a "New Wineskin" (new, but Ancient) that will prayerfully bring much Glory to God is what this book was written to offer to God's People. It is just an offer – you test and see if God could be calling us to such as is contained in these pages, and what your part may be.

church that the gates of hell cannot triumph over at will.[9] We need each other for all of that! Of course we can still fail if we are committed to a course of self-indulgence and don't agape the Truth in our hearts. Adam failed in the "perfect" environment. But our situation is that we have been trying to grow orange trees in Alaska[10] for so long that we have accepted (and built a "theology" to substantiate) the idea that "we're all just weak sinners and one day Jesus will come back and bail us out of our pathetic poverty." Brothers, "it ought not be so!" Jesus came that we could not only experience His Mercy and unwarranted forgiveness, but that we might also "overcome the works of the evil one" and demonstrate His Divine Power by the Spirit that rose Him from the dead![11]

Not everyone is willing to accept a fragmented, powerless life and church, but few know anything else is possible. I received a letter today from a young woman. She wrote of her father, and his search for Truth through the streets of pain and confusion. She found him on the verge of despair and collapse as she spoke with him on the telephone. This is what she said of her conversation with him:

> "He says he goes to church and pretends to worship God with a bunch of other people who pretend to worship God. They chant cliched prayers, take communion, and he walks out with the same undealt-with sins that he walked in with."

---

[9] Ephesians 2:19-22; 1Corinthians 3:9-17, 12:12-31; Romans 12:1-18; 1Timothy 3:15; Matthew 16:18.

[10] The application: Except by God's Sovereign command (that would, as with Paul, bypass the means of Ephesians 4:11-16 and Hebrews 3:12-14), men and women the caliber of Stephen, Philip, Timothy, Silas, Luke, or Priscilla **can not be cultivated in any environment or habitat other than** "daily in public and from house to house," "bearing one another's burdens," "confessing sins one to another," "admonishing one another daily so that none are hardened by the deceitfulness of sin," "when one part of the body suffers, every part suffers with it," etc. Artificial lighting and reading a book on plants to the orange tree will never suffice.

[11] 1John 2:12-14, 5:3-5; Romans 6:5-14, 8:1-39; 2Corinthians 2:14-16, 4:6-18, 6:4-11; Ephesians 1:18-23; 5:25-27; 6:10-18.

God never meant for us to live this way. And there *are* real answers. To find them, we'll need to explore together, and yield to, God's Word and God's Ways. And, above all, we must cry out to the source of the Treasure of "all Wisdom and Revelation" . . . God's Son, Jesus. We need to explore and experience more of both the "Good News of Jesus Christ" and the "Good News of the Kingdom." Together.

Let me take another angle on why we really need to reconsider the entirety of how our recent generations (the last nineteen centuries) have lived out the idea of "church."

Jesus once said: "When a student is fully trained, he becomes like his teacher." He spoke of the catastrophic end of a blind man leading others. And of course, the benefits of following the only One who can see much more than "in the mirror dimly," are obvious. "When a student is fully trained, he becomes like his teacher." Preachers, Pastors . . . the reason for this book is related to this question: "Do you really want all of those who are listening and watching you to turn out just like you?" I contend that no matter who you are, this is far too low a target.

In these last days (according to Jesus, Paul, John, Peter, and the writer of Hebrews), God's Son is the Teacher, the Standard, the Alpha and Omega. The reason it is paramount that we learn to let the King run His Own meetings is that "when a student is fully trained, he becomes like his teacher." I want to help my brothers and sisters learn to walk with Jesus Himself – so that He is their ceiling, not me! I buffet myself that I might be all that I can be for Him with no compromise whatsoever . . . but on my best days, I wouldn't for a minute want to distract any attention away from the One Who "fills everything in every way."

Jesus is not much like me. I am devoted to Him, and desire to radically confront everything in me and around me that is not in His Likeness – but I'm not about to presume to stand up and preside over a group of Believers and give a lecture on this subject or that as if Jesus is far, far away **rather than standing right there with us.**[12] Are you? I want my Family to know HIM, that I might decrease. How about you? Do you wish to stand in for Jesus (by pre-programming the events of a gathering in such a way that He is the topic, but pushed aside, in practice, as the Head of the Church)? Or might it not be worth considering, for the sake of His Lambs and His Name, that Jesus Himself can lead our gatherings "in His Name?"

I would not dare to consciously make myself to be the Standard to "lead men into all Truth," yet if I become the "teacher" because of my "classes," gimmicks, programs, and speeches – those that are subjected to such things will all become "like their teacher." If I've learned, however, to let the King run the meeting, captives can again be "set free." Honestly, Doesn't that sound good?

This crazy idea of risking by turning to Jesus to lead us in gatherings is supremely important! Talking about Jesus and singing about Jesus isn't enough! He's Alive! He really is! He rolled back the stone and galloped out on His white horse, Faithful and True – the Conqueror of sin and death. He's now very much alive and committed to the Headship of a Living Body! We're *not* trying to "use His teachings and methods to get His results." We're taking men to HIM to be discipled! Don't be guilty of leading those around you to be like you through all of the programming and religious choreography (for reasons of insecurity, ambition, or ignorance). If the **Son** sets men free they shall be free indeed! "When a student is fully trained, he becomes like his teacher." Let's all gather *around* Him and not just *for* Him.

(Matthew 23:8-10)
  "You are not to be called 'rabbi,' for you have only one master and you are all brothers. And do not call anyone on earth 'father,' for you have one Father, and He is in Heaven. Nor are you to be called 'teacher,' for you have one 'teacher,' the Christ."

---

[12] I contend that John 14:9-26, Matthew 18:20, and many other similar passages are TRUE! Thank God that they are! Of course speaking to Saints or the unregenerate about Jesus and His Truths is a good thing, but we have seemingly slipped into the world system's way of dealing with things, rather than the Ways of Jesus, through His Father and by His Holy Spirit. Consider it?

This book was meant to provoke and encourage you to go far deeper than perhaps you've been – into the Journey of God the Father, through His Blessed Son, by His Holy Spirit, and with His Family, the saints of God. I want to point you, in practical ways, towards the Adventure of walking **now** in the Light and Love of Eternity, by the Spirit of our Pioneer, Jesus. In His Church.

There's Gonna Be

CHORUS:

When will there be a People
Who cause You more than shame?
When will there be a People
Who do more than borrow Your Name?
When will there be a People
Who undividedly give
Their heart, their soul, their mind and their strength –
Every day that they live?

As I look around the planet
There's not a lot to see.
While many wear the Name of Christ,
We're not a lot like Thee.
We sometimes live to serve ourselves,
Ignoring what you say.
How can we boast we know You
If we don't know Your Way?

CHORUS:

When will there be a People . . .

I lay my life before you
And I trust Your Word is true.
Though my feeble eyes may not have seen,
And my ears may not have heard.
You've said You'd build a Holy Race,
A City set on a Hill.
And if You've said there'd be a People like that –
I trust and know that there will.

CHORUS

Progressive Chorus:

There's gonna be a People . . .
We want to be a People . . .
We're gonna be a People . . .

You're making us a People . . .

Nick

Chapter Two

The Context:
LIFE To The FULL!

W HAT does the Church of Christ Jesus, our current part of the Kingdom of God, really need to look like in order to delight her Betrothed? Let's start with the "Helicopter View" of a daily life together before we touch the details and the substance. What would the Spirit of Christ and a Family of Believers living in obedience to His Word look like in our generation? What does a church today walking in God's Presence and full of Grace look like? How can I recognize the Life of Christ, alive again today in His Body, the Church?

It looks amazingly similar to the Life of Jesus in His physical body two thousand years ago!

Here are twentieth (and twenty-first?) century nurses, restaurant workers, contractors, engineers, teachers, business owners and managers, carpet cleaners, and secretaries – clothed in the garb of the teaching and Life of Jesus; a Church that was formed from His victorious death (Gen. 2:21-22; Rev.5:9; Eph.2:11-22, 5:22-32).

This is typical, natural Life in the Spirit of Christ. This is a touch of the Life God's Family is meant to have – where Truth touches individuals specifically in its gatherings. Meetings are filled with openness, faith-filled confession of sin, teaching, and praise in response to all that is currently happening. Disciples bring songs they've written, praise they're brimming with, chapters from books that have elevated or challenged them, video teaching-tapes that have been a catalyst for growth in them, and ten thousand other possibilities. God's Family is gathered, circled in barns, parks, hotel conference rooms, living rooms, apartment clubhouses, gymnasiums, or stadiums. Every barrier between God's Children is destroyed.[13] This is a small part of the New Covenant, expressed from Acts Chapter 2 to Acts Chapter 2000:

Monday   Early AM... Many of the saints are gathered at different homes to open up their lives to one another before they headed off for work. What was it like? Some laughing; nearly half of the Hebrew letter was read in one of the homes; some passionate prayer for the souls of co-workers; and jubilant praise to Jesus everywhere. Nothing "goo-goo" or hyper-spiritual. Just some rock-solid gratitude to a Living King and terrific friend.

Noon time... Different brothers are together for lunch with each other and some unbelievers with whom they are sharing God's love. Back in the homes, various mothers of young ones are together praying, and encouraging and teaching one another in the challenges of their situations. Practical, challenging time. Some tears are shed, God is honored, and satan is hammered again as the Word of God is spoken into the difficulty. Courage is renewed by **Jesus'** Victory.

Late afternoon... Some disciples are out on a run and meet an unbeliever. He likes the idea of coming over for dinner.

---

[13] In today's version of "church plantings" it is imperative that there be an in-depth study of the culture. Great attention is given to the economic, cultural, and other "valuable" demographics and nuances of the society, with an attempt to appeal to, and not offend, the greatest population groups. Consider how far removed this approach is from anything we read of in the Bible! (Some try to justify it by "verse plucking," but it is only a rather vain attempt to cover over how lacking we are in the fundamentals of walking in God's Life and Power.) All of this is amazingly unnecessary when the nature of the Church is described by eyeball-to-eyeball touching of people's hearts and "laying bare their motives" with Heaven-sent Wisdom. Meeting men's needs and exposing the shadows and fears of the heart span every language and cultural barrier. Keep reading, and you'll see why demographic studies, or "all white," "all black," or "mostly young professional" kinds of churches become a thing of the past when we're really letting Jesus have His Church back.

Evening... Because all the Saints were "seeking first the Kingdom," what started out to be a barbecue with a couple of families and the hungry runner who they found on the running trail at the park, is now 25 people who have found "where God's Action is" this evening. They're sitting in the hallway, up the stairway and into the kitchen as various ones share their hearts and pilgrimage with the newcomer. Prayer and worship are the natural product of the move of God this evening. Of course. "Religion" isn't something we do on some day of the week.[14] It isn't an emotional pacifier, or a

---

[14] There are no "sacred" days in the Christianity of the Bible. Biblically speaking, the "Sabbath" did not move from Saturday to Sunday. Paul actually said he feared he had "wasted his time" on those who still considered one day more sacred than another. In another letter, he allowed for the fact that those with "weaker faith" might still have a holy day, rather than "every day alike," yet that is not God's intention. God spoke of CHRIST as the fulfillment of all special days. Live fully in CHRIST and you will not count one day as more sacred than another; you will not need "holy days" (Col.2:16-17, 20-23; Heb.4, 9:1-10, 10:1; Rom.14:1-5; Gal.3:10-11; etc.). The recorded Biblical history of the first sixty years of the Church of Jesus Christ never mentions holy "seasons" or holy "days" as "Christian" - the church of Christ Jesus and His Apostles did not continue to do such things as they learned to shed the Jewish "shadows" of the "reality that is in Christ." The Biblical record of the Church only even MENTIONS "the first day of the week," or Sunday, TWICE. In sixty years. Is it not true that a record of sixty years of the churches that most are a part of today would have far more than two references to Sunday? Remember, it must be an "orderly account" by a someone like a medical doctor of perhaps apostolic stature, a man such as Luke - the author of the original church record, the Book of Acts. "The Lord's Day" as Sunday, a special day to have a two hour "service," is a shortcut that has replaced the Reality of Christ's Church - we find such a church nowhere in the Scriptures.

For you history buffs, it seems that the concept of "the Lord's Day" as Sunday arose in Ephesus six decades after the Church was born (Christ in the Churches, Logos Tapes, Hazlet, NJ). Interestingly, the phrase "the Lord's Day" only occurs once in the entire New Testament (Rev.1:16), and likely has no reference to a special day of the week even in that instance. Such would be contrary to the very nature of Christianity - the celebration of Life and Reality that fulfill and enlarge the types and shadows of the "externals" in the Old Covenant. The phrase should likely be translated, as it is in every other case (in its Old Testament usage), in the possessive case as "the Day of the Lord" - rather than "the Lord's Day." The entire book of Revelation is, in fact, about "the Day of the Lord," not about "Sunday." What a difference! At least consider the fact that Jesus' Life was never centered around a two hour "service" while He was here, so why should it be now?!

nice little sprig of parsley on the big, important plate of life. Christ and His Kingdom are real. Jesus is now alive, and reigning as the head of a living body – provided we are not disconnected from Him. Consequently, tonight He has used a Priesthood of Believers to do His Will (as He will where we have not denied His Headship by hierarchies, name tags, and pre-programmed liturgy). "And thus the secrets of his heart were revealed; and so, falling down on his face, the non-Christian worshipped God and reported that God was truly among us." And thank Him that He was!

Tuesday   Early AM... Again, especially after last night's cutting-edge time, a number of the Saints are together to seek God's Face. ("My Father's House shall be called a House of Prayer." Without being known for prayer, at least by the Father, it's not *His* House.) This morning, too, one of the women confessed that she was not sharp in the use of her time at home. She earnestly desires some input and a lot of prayer that she might bring her heart joyfully into the Government of God and His Grace. Prayer. Tears. Laughter. Some really excellent time together to start the day.

Daytime... A couple of the men who work third shift have given up some sleep to go from house to house amongst the church and some neighbors doing odd jobs for them. Several non-Christian ladies are over for lunch. Down-to-earth, non-dramatic, God-centered life.

Evening... Two of the men have a strong desire to teach some of the older children some Truths about reverence for our Father and response to His Life and Love in a practical way. The nine of them all head off for a trail through the woods and "rise up, sit down, and walk along the Way" (Deut.11). When they return, they discover that one of the brothers has called the whole church together to share some things that have been stirring in his heart. Some powerful teaching about "the full armor of God." A brother from India who we met in Bombay is visiting with us. He has become a true man of God. He too shared his heart and experience about the weapons and armor of God. All are agreed that we should "declare a Holy Fast" in the church for tomorrow, and really pursue God's application of these Truths to each of our individual lives. *We have Bread that the world knows not of.* (I hope that Bible verse is your experience, as well – to the extent that you could have written it, even if you had never read it?)

Wednesday Early AM... Some on flex-time decide to call in to work and go in a little later this morning in order to join those that would be praying together. The walls, and satan's dominion trembled this morning as we sang the song "The People of God" towards 7:30 . . .

"We're the People of God – called by His Name, called from the dark and delivered from shame. One Holy Race, saints everyone, because of the Blood of Christ, Jesus – the Son!"

Daylight hours... It seems quiet on the home front as most who are home have been apparently seeking out their Father's Love and Word individually. A sister has met a married couple at McDonald's who are nomadic carnival workers. They've received showers and warm food at her home, and I guess they will be with us for a while. Pray for them.

Evening... It started with fifteen or twenty showing up for one of the little guy's Little League games, and then an excursion out for ice cream. The coach came with us, and was drawn up into some profitable conversation about his soul.

As some of the saints were together elsewhere, I understand that it was a frustrating time in some ways. The challenge from Heaven for each of us is to learn to take responsibility for that which God gives us, in gatherings and in our daily walk together. For many,

the years of being a passive audience have taken their
toll, and unlearning that dreadful religious habit
(stained-glass spectacles) sometimes results in awkward
meetings. The beauty of being a family, rather than an
organization, is that we aren't trying to put on a show.
We can talk about stuff like this. In fact, we *live* to talk
about, and draw each other up into, the practical
realization of the highest ways of our Lord, Jesus.

Thursday   Early AM... I assume many were together this morning.
I spent some time at home praying that God would
work in everyone's lives as they met, and as they live
their lives for Him today.

Afternoon... Several of the mothers go to the park with
their children and meet two ladies who live nearby.
One is a Muslim. Jesus was exalted today, and the
Seed of God will not be forgotten. The saints called
quite a number of the others in God's Family at work
and at home. They asked that they pray for Rasili and
Paula while they are at this critical time in the "Valley
of Decision." Tomorrow's time with them should be
revealing.

Evening... Believers gathered, as it happened, in several
homes this evening. At one of the homes, a video
teaching tape was stopped only twenty minutes into the
teaching when a non-Christian had a puzzled look. As
he opened up about his particular confusion, God again
used the Royal Priesthood to speak His Word. One
"had a psalm, another a word of instruction," another a
song. Another had a clear word from Heaven that took
everyone's breath away by it's simplicity and convicting
power. There was little else that could be said, and we
all left quietly, knowing that God had visited His
People. Prayerfully, the non-Christian won't be in that
condition long.

Meanwhile, a few miles away, three brothers and a
sister were sharing Christ and His Kingdom with a
circle of urban tough guys. A "stray" gunshot nearby

drew the attention of the police, resulting in the Saints being frisked alongside of the guys on the street. One of the brothers who wasn't feeling all that guilty got reprimanded for not jumping as quickly as some of the others: "Hey! You in the green shirt. Grab a piece of wall!" Possibly all of this will open some doors, in a backwards sort of way, with the "40th Street Gang." Drugs and violence can't really meet their needs. Our God, Creative as He is (and even with a sense of Humor sometimes), can help us reach them through an avenue that we could never have orchestrated.

Friday   Early AM... I messed up and didn't set my alarm correctly, so I can only say that I know that God's Army and His Truth were surely moving on this morning.

Daytime... It seems like several had the same idea today. Four different people have spent much of the day taking turns watching each other's children as the others read from the prophet Joel. We've all got much to share and so much to learn. But what fun!

Evening... A few of us men are spreading out to various homes to accumulate children in a few places. We'll teach them, love on them, and sing as it seems appropriate, no doubt. (And watch a video with some popcorn, if it seems right at the time! We'll see what happens.) We figure this will also free up the maximum number of parents to have a "Kingdom evening" – an evening where they can get into the homes or streets to do God's bidding.

Saturday   Car repair day today, I guess! The whole church has also enjoyed a cookout together, and some brothers and a few sisters have filled up three basketball courts at a nearby school. The B-ball time was pretty special as one of the guys asked a question about Revelation, Chapter 11 while we were choosing up teams for game four. Forty-five minutes later the large circle of Believers sitting on the blacktop stood back up to continue the "bodily exercise." A good time for the non-

Christians with us as well, though not what they had necessarily bargained for. The only singing most non-Christians are used to during a basketball game is the national anthem!

We didn't expect this as the day was coming to a close, but one of the brothers who was working that evening called a few dozen of us together at 8:30 PM after he got off work. He wanted to confess a trauma from his work place to which he had had a fairly poor response. As others heard of some gathering, more and more poured into the apartment. Calls were made to all ends of the city, everyone moved to the apartment complex clubhouse and grounds, and the children were cared for by those sensitive to see the needs and free up parents. The gathering climaxed sometime after midnight with a Celebration of the Lord's Goodness in breaking the Unleavened Loaf together. I suppose we already had been breaking the Bread of Life much earlier, in a sense. What a fitting finish to such a time. The songs that were on the hearts of God's Elect as different things happened amongst us this evening were enough in themselves to change every life in a four block radius. *"I will build My church, and the gates of hell shall not prevail against it."*

Sunday   We had thought to get together for one of our famous taco salad lunches for the whole church. We did. Six hours later, there wasn't an untouched heart amongst us.

Monday   Early AM... As we gathered in the morning, for some reason only a handful were there. What a treat the others missed! And some say that God doesn't answer prayers about practical things like illness anymore. Tell that to Dave!

Afternoon... A couple of us spent time with a brother who had moved from another city to be with the church here. It seems that his chronic (though

curable!) "stiff neck" is making him and his new
roommates suffer needlessly. Maybe the "root" in his
heart that is driving him is fear, or possibly ambition.
Certainly selfishness. We'll work it out, though. He
seems to desire God's Ways, and that's the best any of
us have to offer. God help us all. What a challenge we
face . . . to learn the Cross, and yet not neglect His
"applied" Righteousness, as we work Truth out together
(Col.1:28; Heb.3:12-14; 1John 3:1-10). Regardless of the
pain, of this we are certain: "I will build my
Community, and the gates of hell shall not prevail
against it!" Jesus *will* overcome . . . in, and through, His
Church! God said so. (Eph.3:10, 20; 1Tim.3:15;
Mat.16:18).

Evening... One of the brothers had called everyone
together this evening. After a little while of trying to
"force" things (of which we repented), we decided that
Jesus doesn't author boring gatherings (it was a real
dud). It was recommended that we needed to go do
something else with our evening. A fairly large
contingent took off for a restaurant, some went to
spend time with people they were reaching out to, and
others went to be alone with their families. It was, in
the end, a nice, peaceful "Kingdom night" – after the
twenty-minute "meeting" was adjourned twenty
minutes too late!

ad infinitum . . . [15]

What religious "category" does this kind of church fit into?
What label would the advocates of the "empty traditions"[16] want
to assign to this kind of life and church? Forget all of the old labels
– they don't work. Truth be known, this is Biblical "Fundamental"
Christianity! This is the kind of "Pentecostal" church that you read
about in the original Acts Chapter Two Pentecost! This is
"Evangelicalism" at its best! This is Christ Jesus – expressed in His

---

[15] The Church Prepared For the Return of Christ.

[16] 1Peter 1:18.

Body in our generation. The corporate Life of Jesus "joined and knit together by every supporting ligament." **This is Church.** A wedge of Light driven by the hammer of God to annihilate the fellowship of darkness. God's Family.

*"I will build **My** Church . . . and the gates of Hell (the powers of the infernal region) shall not overpower it (or be strong to its detriment or hold out against it)."*

*"**Now**, through the **Church**, the manifold, many-faceted, Wisdom of God, in all its infinite variety may be made known to the angelic rulers and authorities (principalities and powers) in the heavenly world."*

*"Now to Him who is able to do exceedingly abundantly above all that we ask or think, according to the power that works in us, to Him be GLORY in the **Church** by Christ Jesus throughout all ages, world without end. Amen."* [17]

Our objective in living, our very reason for drawing breath? For God to get His way on this planet. And, in turn, for Jesus Christ to have a Companion for Eternity – a Spotless, Beautiful Bride, His Church. Can you see it? The Father's Heart, and ours, is a devotion to the Son, *"That He might present to Himself the church in glorious splendor, without spot or wrinkle or any such things, that she might be Holy and blameless!"* [18]

Amen.

---

[17] Matthew 16:18; Ephesians 3:10 (Amplified Version), 3:20.

[18] Ephesians 5:27; Revelation 21:2; 2Peter 3:12a; Acts 3:19-21.

"and much grace was upon them all"
Acts 4:33

We thank you, our Father,
  For what you have done.
Yet it's clear to our hearts
  That you've only begun

To change us and shape us
  And make us brand new
We're thrilled at the thought
  Of what you can do.

For much grace is upon us;
  It's so clear to see
Your gifts undeserved,
  Yet abundant and free.

You've taken a people
  Apart and alone
And knit us together
  And made us Your own.

Imperfect we are;
  That we do not contend.
But aim for perfection
  We will till the end.

For Your grace inspires us,
  Woos us to dare,
To serve with devotion
  Exceedingly rare.

And what of the future?
  For what can we hope?
Far more than survival
  And ability to cope.

The heights we will scale
  And the depths we will probe
Of the love of our Lord
  In majesty robed.

For we serve a God
  Who delights to be known
By those who are willing
  Their lives to disown.

Will we deserve this?
  Oh, never indeed!
But Your grace we'll trust,
  And Your ways will succeed.

All around us there rages
  A war to be won,
And win it we will
  Through the cross of Your Son.

So marshall your forces,
  Dig deeply within,
Seek Jesus inside you,
  Root out every sin.

Take captive the thoughts that
  Distract from the Lord.
Take up the helmet, the shield,
  And the sword.

His glory awaits us;
  Don't ever give in . . .
And with His grace upon us
  We're certain to win.

Kevin

Chapter Three

Priestly Growing Pains

(1Peter 2:4-5)
"As you come to Him, the Living Stone, rejected by men but chosen by God and precious to Him, you also, like living stones, are being built into a house for the Spirit, to be a Holy Priesthood."

(Revelation 1:5-6)
"To Him Who loves us and frees us from our sins by His blood, and has made us to be a Kingdom and Priests - to serve His God and Father, to Him be Glory and Power for ever and ever. Amen!"

L ET me continue to share with you some thoughts about "Church" and "meetings" in the Kingdom of our Lord, Jesus. I've found that one of the toughest things for Believers to do is to figure out how to gather together under the personal oversight of Jesus Christ. How do we gather around HIM, the Master Teacher, rather than simply go through rituals *for* Him (primarily as an audience) on a set day of the week?

There are always some "growing pains" involved in getting from "point A to point B."[19] Since most of us were raised up on

---

[19] A simple, honest survey of the prevailing christian world indicates that most "congregations" consist primarily of a dedicated "core group," surrounded by an environment of those who simply attend a "serve-us" or three. The majority, it is reported, enjoy a potluck dinner occasionally, live a life of relative prayerlessness, regular sin, and worldly priorities. Relationships are usually shallow at best. Most, if put on a lie detector machine, would not be able to say they have any real relationship with Jesus (other than a theoretical one that they've read about). They would not be able to say, with honesty, that they have "rivers of Alive water flowing from their inner man," or that they have ever truly "tasted the Powers of the Coming Age." They do not have a "peace that transcends understanding" or "joy inexpressible and full of Glory." This is the "point A" that most are starting at – missing the very basics of having been born into, and living in, the New Covenant as a child of God!

God's desire, as we have seen, is a People that are together "crushing satan under their feet," "praying without ceasing," living in "fellowship with Him Who is from the Beginning" and "having all things in common." (Heb.3:12-14; Acts 2:36-47;

religious ritual, spiritual gimmicks, and an unbiblical clergy/laity system, learning how to meet together under the Lordship and Teaching of Jesus is just plain awkward sometimes! Though you may think that I'm "nuking a gopher hole," this potential awkwardness is a subject I'll need to address again and again in this time together.

I want to communicate to you here in a practical way so that you will know how to handle the difficulties that arise when you step from ritual to Reality. It's risky! As we grow into Christ's Image individually, and corporately as a Church, some sticky challenges will come up that are never a problem in an institution. A clumsy man sitting in a chair doesn't appear to be clumsy . . . until he stands up and tries to function. Then it becomes very apparent. It is the same in the Church. As long as everything is pre-programmed to ensure that it is "successful" and "spiritual," we will never realize how unspiritual we really are! We will then depart this life thinking that we are something that we are not.

"Meetings" in His Kingdom are to be times when God Himself joins us as we gather with Him, and *each* person functions as a Priest, a vessel of His Love and His Word. As we rise up to take our rightful inheritance as a "Kingdom of Priests," rather than remain an audience, or "laity," we will realize our instabilities and our limitations in a new way! Then we will be able to grow as God desires. In view of this, it is the longing of my heart, and the motivation of this subject having been brought before you now, to prepare you for these clumsy moments with some practical encouragements. Don't allow these early stumblings to discourage you and prompt you to return to a "safer," more comfortable, "risk-free" environment.

Why does it matter? Why can't we just "leave well enough alone" and back-pat everything that calls itself "Christian?" To reiterate a bit, an environment in which men and women remain

---

Eph.5:18; 1Pet.1:8; 1Jn.1:1-8; Jn.17:3, 7:38; Heb.6:4-5; Rom.16:20; Eph.3:10; Mat.16:18; 1Jn.2:14; Jn.6:51; Mat.4:4; 1Jn.3:8, 5:18; Eph.6:10-18, 5:18; Rom.12:11; Jn.14:30; Jas.4:17; 1Jn.3:3-10; Mat.6:33, 13:44-46; Lk.14:33, 9:57-62.)

May God, along with our cooperation, hasten the Journey towards "point B" for the multitudes! For the sake of the Testimony of His Son.

infants for twenty years or more, and hidden sin runs rampant, is in *opposition to God's Will.* I think that's a pretty good reason to ask some questions and make some changes, if we love Jesus.

Oh how it is worth the "growing pains" to lean forward into God's Purposes for your life and church! Stay with me through what could be construed as hard to bear in certain instances. I really don't mean to be obnoxious! Let me give you a glimpse of what is on the other shore, and I'm hopeful that you'll be glad that you were patient with me!

I'd like to address first the heart and practical issues of the small gatherings of God's Family, and later on we'll discuss large gatherings ("daily in **public** and from house to house"), and even multi-city gatherings.

The Greatest Love of All – Kingdom Version

I believe that children are our future.
Teach them well and let them lead the way.
Show them all the beauty they possess inside.
Give them a Rock of Hope – to make it easier. Let the children's honesty
       Remind us how we used to be.

Everybody's searching for a Hero;
People need someone to look up to.
I never found anyone who fulfilled my need.
A lonely place to be – and then I found the loving Prince of Peace.

I decided long ago to live for Him who makes me whole.
When I fail, when I succeed, I can press on because I'm freed.
No matter what they take from me, they can't take away my destiny...
Because the Greatest Love of all is happening to me;
I found the Greatest Love of all inside of me.
The Greatest Love of all is easy to achieve;
Learning to love the SON – it is the Greatest Love of all.

I believe that children are our future.
Teach them well and let them lead the way.
Show them all the beauty they possess inside.
Give them a Rock of Hope – to make it easier. Let the children's honesty
       Remind us how we used to be.

I decided long ago to live for Him who makes me whole.
When I fail, when I succeed, I can press on because I'm freed.
No matter what they take from me, they can't take away my destiny...
Because the Greatest Love of all is happening to me;
I found the Greatest Love of all inside of me.
The Greatest Love of all is easy to achieve;
Learning to love the SON – it is the Greatest Love of all.

And you should know that special place that you've been dreaming of
Leads you to the Risen King . . . find your strength in HIM.

Adapted, *Mike*

Chapter Four

Jesus IS Still Alive!

(1 Corinthians 14:24-26)
"But if all prophesy, and an unbeliever or an uninformed person comes in, he is convinced by all, he is judged by all. And thus the secrets of his heart are revealed; and so, falling down on his face, he will worship God and report that God is truly among you. How is it then, brethren? Whenever you come together, each of you has a psalm, has a teaching, has a tongue, has a revelation, has an interpretation. Let all things be done for edification."

THE Principles of *Letting the King Run the Meeting* are the same no matter what the size of the gathering, whether two or two hundred thousand (though we may discover some different twists when we get there)! All of the "principles" revolve around this one Truth: THE GRAVE IS EMPTY! JESUS IS ALIVE. HE IS THE HEAD OF HIS CHURCH! Hallelujah.

Now, how does that change things? What does it mean for the Body to submit to the current direction of her Head? How would the King of the Church reign in reality in the meetings of His Church (rather than merely in philosophical theory)? Reason with me a moment.

Does it not make sense that if Jesus is still alive, and the Head of the Church is **present** when "two or three are gathered in His Name,"[20] that we would let Jesus run the meeting? Can you imagine Peter, James, Andrew, and the others sitting in rows and files for two hours, a day or two each week, doing "studies" about Jesus, when He was right there with them? Do you suppose that they decided a month in advance what they were going to do when they were with Jesus? . . . Or do you think that possibly they let Jesus decide the agenda when they were together? You know they were just simply committed to be *with* Him, and to let Him set the sails!

---

[20] Matthew 18:20.

Imagine you are in a church building next Sunday that functions in ceremonies, rather than Reality. Just as you slide the hymnal back into the rack after the opening song, the booming voice of Gabriel cracks the plaster with these words:

"We now interrupt the 'regularly scheduled program' to bring you a message from the King of Kings and Lord of Lords . . . ":

Jesus declared, "Believe me, a time is coming when you will worship the Father neither on this mountain nor in Jerusalem, [at a certain prescribed time and a certain prescribed place] . . . . Yet a time is coming and has now come when the true worshipers will worship the Father in spirit and truth, for they are the kind of worshipers the Father seeks. God is spirit, and his worshipers must worship in spirit and in truth."

The Christianity, the New Covenant, that we read of in the Bible, has always been intended by God to be limitless in its expression!

If I might be so bold as to ask, I'd like you to pray fervently tonight and in the days to come about the magnitude and the ramifications of the Truths (if these are truly the ways of Christ Jesus) we are about to discuss. If you are earnestly desiring reality rather than theory and academics, please be open to hearing, and even fasting, over the *application* of any Truth that may follow, *to your own personal life and church.* This is not about a gimmicky, informal alternative to ritual (PLEASE!),[21] but about the freedom that we have to be Family in Christ. We need not continue to be entranced and constrained by a stiff, regulated, religious environment entirely foreign to the Church that Jesus established – the one that we read of in the Bible. **Many of you already know**

---

[21] 1Cor.11:17-34 makes it clear that, while they had no "services" as most have known them (1Cor.14:26) per se, they certainly were to take their time together in gatherings in a very serious way. Let's not be careless, but rather respect God's Oracles as Paul said the Thessalonians had. They received God's Word through His vessels "not as the words of men, but as it actually is, the Word of God" . . . "with power, with the Holy Spirit, and with deep conviction." With that attitude, we'll do fine!

only too well how dangerous this vacuum of true Life can be for marriages, teenagers, and all of our lives together.

Let's just touch on some of the attitudes we need to cultivate in understanding this extraordinary topic (of meeting together with the unseen Head of the Church and Creator of the Galaxies), and also discuss a few practical considerations that will come up as we do meet together in Him.

As we consider the nature of meetings of His Church, we must give much weight to the glimpse of meetings in the New Testament Church found in Paul's first letter to his Family in Corinth, chapter 14:24-26. This segment of his letter to the brothers and sisters in the city of Corinth describes a meeting in the church of which they were a part. In their gathering, even though the church was very weak in many respects, an unbeliever could still fall on his face and cry out "God is really among you!" Why would he fall on his face? Because God really WAS among them in the gathering of the saints. THAT in itself seems to be a key missing ingredient in the church of this generation.

While religious and emotional hype at some religious meetings might have a similar appearance to God's presence on a temporary basis, "by its fruit you shall know it." Lives, families, work places, and neighborhoods aren't permanently altered by simply an "uplifting worship experience." The following truths about gatherings and honesty before God WILL have that impact. Why? Because change is based on these words of Jesus: "You shall know the Truth, and the Truth shall set you free" (John 8:31-32; Rom.12:1-2).

Hopefully I'll be able to communicate, as we continue, how the nature of gatherings has a tremendous impact on the speed of Spiritual growth in God's People. Being a true Priesthood, rather than an audience, is not an unimportant, optional nicety!

Some of what I'm about to say will be meaningful to those whose orientation is towards accepting prophecy to be part of the New Covenant and God's Church, but possibly not as meaningful to those who believe that this element was only for the first century Church. Either way, let's stick together and work through some Biblical principles.

The passage in 1Corinthians, Chapter 14, that mentions the non-Christian man collapsing in the Presence of God in the church gathering also mentions prophecy. Is prophesying the element that caused the unbelieving man to fall on his face and cry out *"God is truly among you?"* Prophecy is not the issue really. "Prophesying" is added in some churches today because this element is in the framework of their belief system, and so they must therefore have prophesying in the assembly in order to please God. This reasoning may seem to be correct at first glance, but the fact that something may be Biblically possible and valuable doesn't necessarily mean that God is going to do it on cue. Frequently prophecy today is somewhat conjured or forced (though usually, no doubt, by sincerity or peer pressure, not ambition). Even when the prophecy seems impressive at the moment, it often proves ultimately to be powerless and false by the test of time. For those who honestly care about Truth more than reputation, faddish prophesying should be lovingly exposed as only an imitation of the real thing. "The emperor has no clothes." Unchallenged, broken "prophetic" promises, carnal expression by carnal men, and lack of fruit as the years roll by, all testify that our desires can sometimes overshadow our discernment. Let's deal honestly (though never cynically or skeptically – 1Thes.5:19-20) with what we are hearing today. God can stand up to investigation. If our hearts are soft and teachable, He will show us, in His time, the real thing.[22]

---

[22] Now don't get mad at me! If there is a chance that I can cause some of my Family to stop and consider some things that would be helpful, though possibly painful, even at the risk of my (non-existent) reputation and favor with some, it would be worth it. I don't want to not be liked, but I've got to take that chance! I'm compelled! Here goes. Please consider God's Word as you consider the fate of conjuring up prophesying in the assembly to "keep up with the Smith's":

(Deuteronomy 18:20-22)
    "A prophet who presumes to speak in my name anything I have not commanded him to say, or a prophet who speaks in the name of other gods, **must be put to death.**"
    You may say to yourselves, "How can we know when a message has not been spoken by the Lord?"
    "If what a prophet proclaims in the name of the Lord does not take place or come true, that is a message the Lord has not spoken. That prophet has spoken presumptuously. Do not be afraid of him."

If we really were planning on obeying God, we would have a lot of dead "prophets" to bury. We couldn't be applauding, with God's Mind, those who are

The biggest problem that we have had in recent generations is not really so much related to prophesying. The real problem is the fact that God just plain hasn't been among us much at all in the majority of religious activities in this generation. If the Creator of the Cosmos showed up in the room, would it be noticeable? Me thinks so.[23] How? Rest assured: God will make His Presence

---

speaking of "60-80% accuracy." I'm not advocating murder, but just trying to communicate to you the severity of God's Judgment on men "stealing from one another [or begetting from their imaginations] words supposedly from Me" (Jer.23). One "miss" is sufficient to end the streak permanently, if we are willing to follow God, rather than bandwagons. I don't mean to sound harsh – I don't know how we are going to bridge the gap of "vacuum to reality" without making mistakes, either. How were **they** to bridge that gap in the passage in Deuteronomy just quoted? Yet it says what it says: "Kill those who prophesy what does not come to pass." God will just have to help us, I guess! In the mean time, we don't need to strain to make something happen out of the flesh, out of ambition, or out of desperation and impatience.

I know, from what I've seen and from those that I'm close to, that skeptics and advocates of Acts 2:17-18 alike are not completely convinced by all that is happening today. It seems clear that those in authority in groups that affirm 1Cor.14:1 are frequently unconvinced that a "prophecy" is from Heaven. Many times those who are directing the assembly to achieve the best effect (as they were admittedly taught to do in Seminary) will interrupt a questionable spontaneous prophetic utterance when the one prophesying pauses for a breath. This scenario has occurred in innumerable places: the Pastor or Worship Leader quickly leads a song or adds a few remarks in order to slickly cover up the embarrassing problem with the prophecy, or the things that he did not want the flock to hear.

Maybe we should even reconsider our prior ideas of the means in which prophesying was done in the early apostolic church. True prophesying may not be as stained-glass and lofty and **uninterruptible** as most of us have thought (read 1Cor.14:30). Prophecy is likely to be, in its highest form, very organic and natural. Though powerful and nearly unbelievable in its piercing riches, true prophecy is often as innocent and genuine as the Carpenter lovingly looking you right in the eye and revealing your heart. Contrast that with (1) a guru in a trance; (2) an angry, tuft-haired, eccentric man with projectile saliva; (3) a flashy flatterer with much personal boasting; he maybe leads a "mutual back-patting society" with those in leadership wherever he goes; or, (4) a timid lamb that musters the courage to try to make a simple heart conviction sound like a prophecy in a gathering. Such children we are! It's a good thing He loves us so much . . . ! By His grace, we ARE going to make it!

[23] There will be times, of course, where God challenges us to faithfulness without a lot of feedback. The Israelites got into a heap of trouble for complaining

known, and in any way He sees fit. He will lay bare the motives and the intentions of mens' hearts in any way He sees fit. The essential ingredient we desire is that He really *would be* among us.

(1 Corinthians 5:4)
>   *"When you are assembled in the name of our Lord Jesus and I am with you in spirit, and the power of our Lord Jesus is present . . . ."*

The environment referred to in the passage quoted in 1 Corinthians 14, the gathering in which He's really among us, at work in His Priesthood of Believers, looks like this:

>   *"When you come together everyone has a hymn or a word of instruction or a revelation . . . ."*

Though this kind of freedom in gatherings will not guarantee God's involvement in them, this is the nature of gatherings of the Church recorded in, and responding to, the Bible. This freedom in meetings, rarely with an official "leader" other than Jesus Himself, is an essential ingredient of a Family of Believers consistent with God's Intent – a Priesthood rather than spectators. We must not yield to the gentiles' format for "order": a few selected (or hired) men performing for and motivating an "audience" in a "same bat time, same bat place" kind of structure.

The clearest picture we have of the New Testament Church meeting in the Bible involves people coming together with each member of Christ's Body having "considered how"[24] to spur the Family on. ALL are to be the priests of God – the priesthood of believers bringing songs, and words of instruction, and revelation.[25]

"Is God among us or not?" (1Cor.10:10). Yet, all in all, the marks of a Church whose Existence was born in Heaven, in the "Power of an Indestructible Life," should be plentiful. Not just theoretical.

[24] Hebrews 10:24-25.

[25] In case you're wondering, "decently and in order," in its context in 1Corinthians, chapter 14, does not mean a prescribed liturgy of two songs, a prayer, a sermon, etc. It includes, in the same paragraph, "everyone brings a song, a word of instruction." That is "decent and in order"– if the King Himself is directing the time. If He's not, we may need to strike these 1 Corinthians 14 Truths about "how

Again, the practice of Jesus' Church did not, and does NOT, as God is allowed His Way, include a hired Bible teacher standing behind a pulpit or even informally in front, giving a "lesson" to an audience that's watching a pre-arranged, pre-programmed, planned chain of religious events.[26] It NEVER was that way when Jesus and men that knew Him were around. NEVER. Yet it is the pattern today in more than 999 out of 1000 religious organizations. No one, scholar or otherwise, has ever found our modern-day pre-arranged kind of environment described anywhere in the New Testament. And our loss for having settled into departmentalized religion is immeasurable.

To illustrate in a playful way the silliness of our state, apart from a much-needed restoration . . .

Just picture this scene happening in a cave in the first century: a little shingle titled "Visitor's Sunday" is positioned just outside of the cave. The congregants file in quietly, dressed in their finest apparel, and find their habitual seats on rocks carefully placed in rows and columns on the floor of the cave. Ushers are available to help the visitors find a rock suitable to their financial standing. Two songs and a prayer start the program. The master of ceremonies helps to navigate the "worshippers" through the defined sequence of "orderly" spiritual components. (Some caves on different street corners are more expressive than others, but it comes out about the same.) A carefully prepared speech is delivered by the

---

to function in the gatherings" from our Bibles. It is truly too risky to live this way if men are separate from the Head. We will have chaos if there is no script to follow, no Master of Ceremonies to keep the meeting rolling, and Jesus is not running the meeting. "Every man does what is right in his own eyes" when there is "no King." A script, and traditions of men, are the way to go if Jesus isn't at the meeting and giving the direction!

[26] Is a freedom in Charismatic assemblies for any to prophesy or bring a "word of knowledge" at some specified time during the "service" really bringing forth the "layman" into his place as a priest of God? It seems that this generally misses the mark. First of all, it is only allowed in a specified (spoken or unspoken) segment of time. While this seems to allow more freedom for the Family than the traditional denominational setting allows, it still falls short of what God is after. God and His priesthood are still limited to performing within the limits set by folkways and mores, or by those that are orchestrating the gathering. We must learn to let Jesus reign, and TRUST Him!

speaker of the hour. Some singing, or "fellowship time" ends the day's events. Paul, Peter, or whoever the dignitaries might be, position themselves at the mouth of the cave to shake parishioners' hands after the "service" and set up any counseling appointments that the congregants might request.

Is that the way that you have it pictured? We all know better. It didn't happen then, and it mustn't happen now.

If it's not to be the pre-fabbed, packaged plan of "services," what should our gatherings look like instead? In the Book of Acts, we see some principles about New Testament meetings. In Acts 20, for example, we remember the power of God having been displayed in a young man named Eutychus. As the gathering went on hour after hour *until dawn,* ultimately, Eutychus fell asleep, fell three stories from his informal place on the window sill, died, and was raised from the dead. What a night![27] That's the nature of things. It began with a gathering that was not sterile choreography centered around a speech to dressed-up folks sitting in pews, for a pre-determined length of time. Paul did not give a long-winded "sermon" as some might have thought. He "dielegeto" (Greek) – *dialogued* with them in someone's home!

In Corinth, when no one of Paul's stature was present, things did not grind to a boring halt. Nor did they find someone to "fill in" as the resident "man of God." As we have seen, **God has always wanted a "Holy Nation" of priests** (see Exodus 19:4-6), not a few Levites to deliver sermons, lead singing, and make decisions. They were to be a Royal Priesthood. In the Church of the New Covenant, that finally came to pass (Jer.31:31-34; Ezek.36:24-32; Heb.8:8-13). And when they met together, they met as if they were now *all* Priests! And as if their precious Lord was still Alive!

He is.

---

[27] They all had jobs they had to get up for the next morning, children to consider, and the normal responsibilities of life that we face as well. But they, as a challenge to us, knew how to "seek first the Kingdom." What blessings we miss when we walk by sight, "the logical," and not by faith!

You Alone

Father, I thank you
for giving Christ to me!
And, Father, please help me be
another son willing
to die for Thee.

CHORUS
For You alone are
Worthy to be praised!
And Your grace
is sufficient for me.
For in my weakness
Your power is made whole;
and so it shall be
for all Eternity!

Jesus, I thank you
for giving Life to me!
And Jesus, I give you
back the life you
freely gave to me.

CHORUS

Spirit, I thank you
for BEING Life in me!
And Spirit, please others seek
to live inside and
so to set them free!

CHORUS

Chris

Totally You

There was a new Life
Waiting our there for me.
There was a breakthrough
That I couldn't see.
I could trust You with each moment
Till my life was brand-new,
And, Lord, when it happened it was totally You,
totally You.

<u>CHORUS</u>
'Cause no power on earth it could be.
No power on earth could set me free.
So I'll proclaim it to the nations;
I'll shout it from the roof;
My life will be the witness;
They'll need no other proof.
It is totally You,
totally You.

I won't lay back and waste your time, Lord,
I've got dying to do.
And even as I'm dying,
There are lives to press into.
Lord, You've got the new Life;
I know Your promises are true.
And, Jesus, with each victory, it's totally You,
totally You.

<u>CHORUS</u>

Patty

Jesus

... a song

Jesus Christ is my King and my Master
He's the Lord of my Life to the end.
He's the Holy One of God, and I love Him.
He's the One who set me free from all my sin.

On the cross there He had His great heart broken,
Carried out the Father's will unto the end.
Where I go now, my friends, you can't go with me;
But I prepare a place for you, and I'll come again.

Love each other the same way that I have loved you;
To my Father and myself you must be true,
Then we'll work and live in you through the Spirit,
To show the world the Son of God, living in you.

Jesus Christ, Lamb of God and my Savior,
King of Kings, Cornerstone, Almighty God,
Lord of Lords, the I Am and Messiah,
And Your love is our guide and chastening rod.

If we walk in the Light all our life long,
Then we'll be that city set upon a hill,
Shining His light of love to a dark and dreadful kingdom,
Drawing men to praise His name around God's throne

Jenny

The Greatest Love Story*

There is a man and God, one and the same, who died for me because I am unworthy to be loved with a perfect love.

He scanned the universe, and then, with a tenderness in His eyes reached down and drew me unto Himself. He told me that He loved me and offered to me to receive His perfect love, explaining that He alone was worthy to offer it to me.

With gladness I took it and gave Him mine, forsaking all others who would court me or attempt to turn my head from the One who would now forever hold me.

How handsome my Lover is O How handsome! His eyes are like flames of fire. His hair is as white as wool, His feet like brass and His voice like the sound of many waters, like the sound of a multitude.

How beautiful my beloved is! O how beautiful! In her mouth do I entrust my words. Her lips drip honey. She is dressed for battle. She lives to love Me and see My work done. Her feet are shod with preparation that comes with the gospel of peace. She is adorned with jewels. And it is still yet to be seen all that she will be.

It is You, my Lover, who adorns me with jewels. It is You who brought me up from the pit of my despair. You make me to walk beside the still waters. You restore my soul. You clothe me in Your righteousness. You lead me in the paths of righteousness for Your name's sake. And all Your ways are pure. You anoint my head with oil My cup overflows.

My lover is mine and I am His. What God has joined together let not man nor principalities nor any force separate.

Let the King take me into His chambers behind the curtain. For He has taken me as His own.

My lover is mine and I am His. And it will be so forever.

*This is a true story. And you can live in the reality of it as well.

Lesli

(Rev.1:14-16; Eph.6:15; Ps.23; Rom.8:38-39; Matt.19:6; Song of Solomon; ad infinitum)

Chapter Five

A Prepared Life

T O recap, because we are *all* to be Priests before God,[28] with
Jesus Himself as the Head of His Church, the gatherings will
need to reflect this Truth. With no spiritual apartheid, every
member of the Body of Christ will be free to offer to the rest of
God's People the Life with which Jesus is filling them. In God's
most fruitful Work, this will not include a spiritual equivalent of
"Bob Barker" or "Donahue" directing traffic and controlling.

*"You are not to be called leader (NAS, or teacher, or father) for
you are all brothers, and have but one, the Christ."* [29]

As a couple of Church historians have remarked regarding the
church that Jesus has started:

"The fellowship was an organism rather than an
organization. The members had a common experience.
They were fused. They were baptized into one Spirit.
They ate a community meal, all partaking together of
one loaf, and all together drinking of one cup . . . .
There was no rigid system. 'Custom' laid no heavy
hand on anyone. Routine and sacred order had not yet
come. There was a large scope for spontaneity and
personal initiative. Persons and gifts counted for
everything. Procedure was fluid and not yet
standardized . . . . The fellowship was more like a
family group than like the church, as we call it.
Everything was unique, and nothing repeatable. No
leader dominated the group gatherings. The body met
as a community of the Spirit; and, as Paul said, 'where
the Spirit is, there is Liberty'– not bondage or routine."

---

[28] There are particular gifts that God has given to different members of the
Body of Christ that manifest themselves in different ways. We'll talk more about
this in the chapter on leadership, and elsewhere along the way.

[29] Matthew 23:5-15.

"The one single characteristic of apostolic worship and life was truly its spontaneity. The resurrected Christ was simply free to be Himself, by the power of the Holy Spirit, in His Church! In His Body He freely moved and had His Being - again in marked contrast to what we shall see develop in the ensuing centuries." [30]

One hundred years ago, another had written of the fluidity of the Christianity of the Bible, the Church that Jesus began. He wrote, "The gift and guidance of the freely-moving Holy Spirit was the only valid, original Church order." [31]

Now, all of this is well and good. Yet even before any gathering of God's Saints might be considered, we should address a preliminary issue. If this issue I'm about to mention is not in order, anything we might say about letting Jesus Himself, in all of His Glory and Wisdom, direct the gathering, will be relegated to the imaginary and emotional. There is a prerequisite for knowing how to walk with Christ and letting Him reign in a meeting of the Elect. Ready? The first question must be this:

Who are *you?* To whom does your life belong, *really?* (Probably your family, co-workers, and your checkbook stubs would confirm your appraisal of yourself?) Because the Kingdom is "neither here nor there, but within you," it is of no use whatsoever (in fact it will be rather dangerous!) to have a "different kind of meeting" to replace the old . . . unless your own personal life reflects a current response to the current Lordship of Jesus.

---

[30] Rufus M. Jones; Root Out of Dry Ground, Schmitt. See also Acts, God; and with varying degrees of usefulness: The Pilgrim Church, Broadbent; The Torch of the Testimony, Kennedy; The Spreading Flame, Bruce; The Early Church, Frend; The Rise of Christianity, Frend; Letter to Diognetus, second-century writing; The Early Christians, (Die ersten Christen nach dem Tode der Apostel), Arnold; Church History, Shelley; The Early Church, Chadwick; Church Adrift, Matthew; Thy Kingdom Come, Baxter; Nicolaitanism - the Rise and Growth of Clergy, Grant; The New Testament World in Pictures, Stephens.

[31] Kirchenrecht, Vol.1, Sohm.

If you are not walking in Fellowship with, and under the Government of, the Holy Spirit continually as a way of life, then don't get excited about a chance to have some "loose format." That is not the issue at all! **What I am attempting to share with you has everything to do with reality in the inner man, and destroying everything that stands in the way of that, and nothing to do with "informality" in gatherings.** *The "meetings" will take care of themselves* when a Body of Believers are dedicated to living radically and obediently, by Faith, for Jesus 24-hours-a-day, and they are "compacted together" in His way.[32] Start by dealing a death blow to selfishness, fear, laziness, gluttony, materialism, job or family or entertainment idolatry, legalism, boastfulness, shyness, talkativeness, gossip, religious pride, and the rest of the assortment of sins that come between ourselves and our Father. Any change in "meeting format" is a bad gimmick if the reality "within you" is not present. Start there!

And then, when the Church meets together, and you've come with a prepared life to the gathering of His People, you will come with your heart already toward God. Be mentally fruitful and prayerfully desirous of giving God honor all day long, and your part as a responsible brother or sister in a meeting will be a cinch. Lay down your life in humility and honesty, being sensitive to others' needs. All of a sudden, God's Word takes on meaning when it says, "Consider how you might spur one another on to love and good works." This will not be just THEORY for a life that is *truly* prepared in Christ Jesus!

When you do come together as the people of God, don't just wander in like you're going bowling or something. As in all circumstances of your day, have your life so hidden in Christ that you are keenly aware of all that is at stake in the Spirit in the lives of those that are at the gathering of the Saints. Be vigilant! If two or three are gathered in His Name and "there He is in their midst," then the reigning King and Creator of the universe is in the room! Of course, we are always in His Presence if we are walking in fellowship with Him. Yet there is something special, according to Jesus, when His Body is gathered in His Name.

---

[32] Apostolic Foundations and Apostolic Patterns.

Would you come before any mere president or earthly king dazed by your own little world, or would you "consider" [33]with mature thinking the meaning of this time with him? You know that answer!

Sometimes in a gathering we may have ten minutes of total silence. (Though this is rare for us, even in Heaven it can happen – Rev.8:1.) If this were to happen, unplanned, where you are, how would you feel? If you KNEW Jesus was sitting in your midst, you would not be uncomfortable in the least. Nor would you be concerned for "what the visitors thought." That would be Jesus' concern. For you (as long as it wasn't due to empty hearts), it would simply be some precious time with your Lord. It's okay to sit at His feet, as Mary did! Slow down, Martha! Yet, if you were not inclined to recognize the Presence of Jesus when "two or three are gathered in His Name," you would likely be bored or nervous or judgmental. If you *did* Know that the Creator of the galaxies was sitting in your room, that ten minutes of silence would be tremendous!

Here's what I'm saying: come with your life and your heart toward God and prayerfully desirous of giving God honor. Be bent on laying down your life for Him and others. Be humble, honest, and sensitive to others' needs. And maintain an awe of God Almighty, in gatherings of the Saints and anywhere you are!

As your heart is prepared, so also should your mind be prepared. But not in the way the world does such things . . . .

---

[33] Hebrews 10:24-25.

Chapter Six

Overflow of Life,
Not Concepts

I F you have found that looking at the backs of people's heads is not the way you would communicate in your home, then it will become more and more obvious to you as you ponder these things that it is not the way to express ourselves in God's Family (in "pews" or whatever), either. We are then faced with the dilemma of "What *should* happen instead of the only way that we know?!" If you are ready to live as a Priest or Priestess of God and do the Work of God in a gathering of His Elect, then you are, no doubt, wondering how to function. If we set aside the planned liturgy, what is left? How does one walk in what the Bible speaks of as, "When you come together, everyone has a song, a Word of instruction, a revelation" without chaos? In other words, "What does a gathering look like when the Living Jesus is allowed to steer and address and instruct His own assembled followers?" [34]

As one in a Priesthood, no longer a "spectator" at "services," how do you become a contributor and not just an observer in a gathering? One essential practical issue is this: as you read, study or listen to the word of our God outside of the meeting, never listen or read "to share," but only to be *changed.* The way of God is this: no matter how profound the Truth you have heard or learned happens to be, He only truly values the work of those who are currently *applying* the Word of God to their lives. Please take the time to let this sink deeply into your heart and mind. This is so crucial! He can only overflow from your life if you "abide" – make

---

[34] Contrast that idea with an overstated but painfully real modern-day scenario: "a group of folks meeting in His memory to study His life and teachings and bide time until Heaven." I have a personal preference between those two possibilities! How about you?!

your dwelling place – in Him and His Word. Your words will be His if He is filling who you *are* and you are storing up His Life in a trusting and obedient heart.

In the parable of the soils,[35]Jesus speaks of being obedient and responsive to the words of God. Essentially, as we uproot the cares of the world and the deceitfulness of riches from our lives, God can give the increase to His Word in our lives. In accordance with our faithfulness with the seeds, God will (vs. 26-28), "we know not how," give increase through us, 30, 60, or 100-fold. We don't know how, but as we plant the seed and go to bed at night, the life of God somehow sprouts forth. It's not a matter of being eloquent, talented or intellectually well-equipped in methodology. Rather, He calls us to *obey* the Word of God.

In essence then, all of the "great concepts" that you may study are nothing but chaff if you're not applying them to your own life. Do not read, look at, and listen to things *in order to* share with others. That's not how God does the supernatural work of transforming other people's lives. He will use us 30, 60, or 100-fold *if* we're obedient to God and listening for His word to change our *own* lives.

Our job is to be drunk with the Holy Spirit and filled to the brim with the Life and Stature of Christ. Then God will use the overflow to reach others. Fill your cup with obedience and the pursuit of God – listening for the Rhema of God that you might apply Truth to your own heart. Read God's Word for application to your own heart . . . not so you might have something to say at a meeting, or to someone else. You may ultimately share what you have learned, but not as the "man of the hour," the assigned "teacher" or the "star orator." Instead, you might share Truth as another member of the Family, with God's Truth digested in your heart and now manifested for the good of all.

Truth applied to your heart will overflow, if you are prepared, in God's timing. Someone may say something or confess a sin, a song may be sung, or a scripture read, and it will trigger the life of God in you to well up and burst forth. True Life won't come from

---

[35] Mark 4:14-20, 26-29.

some kind of planned, intellectual "neat" thing that you wanted to share with people. It will come out of the overflow of your life that's "hidden in Christ."

If your life really does belong to Him . . . *then* release it! Once you have met Jesus face-to-face on the matter at hand, as far as you are able, then come on ahead! Bring the gifts of the songs you have written to, or for, Jesus! Share the poems that you have written to your Lord or to your brothers and sisters. Read aloud to the Elect Ones the chapter from the book you are reading that "lit your fire!" Read the Book of Romans together out loud if it has recently been burning in your heart, and the others agree that it is a good time to do that. Is there a dramatic play that you have seen in your mind's eye that you could enlist the help of some Family to offer as a gift to the Saints, and your Savior? Fill your heart, and go for it!

Chapter Seven

"You Ought To Be Teachers By Now," or "Not Many Teachers?"

(Hebrews 5:12; James 3:1)

T HERE seems to be a conflict between these two Scriptures, does there not? Let's continue on the course we have set, and see if these two passages do not harmonize readily in the context of organic, rather than institutional, Life.

REFINED BY FIRE

This key question re-stated: What do you share of what you've learned? Are the gatherings now to be "free for all," a chaotic gab-fest? A "pooling of ignorance" (known affectionately among us as "P of I")? Certainly not. That kind of thing makes for some worthless gatherings. Some of us know this first-hand, for sure!

What then do we share? How do we know what is chaff thrown on the mountain of words and what is from God for His People? How do we walk in the Ways of our Lord who "said nothing that He did not hear His Father saying?" How do we speak "as the very oracles of God?"

First of all, share what has "become flesh" in you.[36] Share those things that have impacted your life in a dramatic way – not just "neat" concepts gleaned from a cassette tape of the latest fad ministry. Nor the borrowed-from-the-commentators wisdom of the "junior-scholars" that is so prevalent in churchianity "Bible classes." Often it will be months before any Truth is part of you (Truth that has "become flesh" in you), rather than only in your head. Wait. Maybe as a Truth becomes alive to you, it will be a full six months of absolute, total silence about this facet of Truth before you speak to anyone except God alone on the issue. Be cautious of a shallow way of life: learning something and immediately spilling it all out when you come together. Have you really petitioned God for the full impact and application of this Truth? Be wary of Ephraim's half-baked cake.

In my own personal experience, a few years ago I remember being swept off my feet (in a good way) by some prayer-closet enlightenment about, "As many as are lead by the Spirit are Sons of God." The significance of that critical Truth's relationship to one of its spiritual shadows, the "Tree of Life," was shocking and Life-giving to me. It literally undermined my whole engineer's and attorney's approach to Christianity and the Bible. I was travelling on the East coast some time after I had begun praying about all of this, and began sharing some things about the tree of life with a preacher out there. He excitedly asked me, "How long have you been learning about the 'Tree of Life' versus 'the tree of the knowledge of good and evil?'" I replied that it had been over a year since I'd *begun* to learn to eat from the "Tree of Life" and to despise (as God does) the "tree of the knowledge of good and evil." Even so, it was months after that before I could put words on it to even mention it to anyone else. At that point I had *still* never expressed it, except in passing, in the church of which I am a part. (Occasionally, as the Saints were together en masse or in homes, I had mentioned that sometime I hoped to share some things that the Father was doing in me out of Genesis 3, Galatians 5, Romans 8, and some other

---

[36] Jesus was, and is, the perfect manifestation of all that God believes and values (Hebrews 1:1-3; Colossians 1:13-20). He was the first of a new race, the "Firstborn." "The Word became flesh and dwelt for a while among us." Though our lives are not yet fully transformed by His Word, that is the objective we have determined to pay any price for! We, too, want to have the Father's Word manifested (not just quoted or studied) in our lives by His Spirit.

passages. I'd offer a few thoughts to my brothers and sisters, and then I'd prayerfully let the subject trail off.)

The reason I didn't just "dump the load" from the top of my head was that "the word was becoming flesh in me;" I was just beginning to understand it in deeper and deeper ways. By the time I first shared about this communion with the Father, the direction of His Spirit, and the Tree of Life in a little more depth in Dallas, my words were coming out of the overflow of probably hundreds of hours with Him and in His Word about this. Rather than scraping for words and manufacturing thoughts to fill in the holes, I was sharing my experience as easily as an eye-witness could describe a precious birth.

Even then, I would not have shared those thoughts, except we had had a powerful evening the night before with a group of Christians that vowed that they would change their lives and repent of the materialism and shallowness that had marked their earlier lives. I was torn as I prayed later that evening and concluded that if they were serious in their hunger to go into the "Most Holy Place" then they needed to know that they could never get there by simply studying their Bibles more, in an intellectual way. Many thousands of people know their Bibles and couldn't be further from knowing Jesus in intimacy. Can anyone relate?

You may be able to see (from some of these thoughts about sharing cautiously from the "overflow") how to resolve the dilemma of "Not many of you should be teachers" and "You should all be teachers by now."

These problems (of "not many teachers" versus "you ought to be teachers by now") are good "problems" to have. The vast majority of Christians have been raised up in a Lifeless (though possibly very busy) church situation where they are never required to do much that isn't on a cue card for them, or presented to them on the silver platter of a program. What a tragedy!

But, here is the other side. With your new-found freedoms to be more than an audience, or a puppet on a string, come the possibilities of making mistakes such as the one we have been speaking of: "talking off the top of your head."

Teaching when we have but shallow *experience* with Christ is
a bit like taking a cup that's half full and trying to share something
out of it. We can shake it real hard to get something from it, but
instead it ends up being a sloppy mess. Have you had the experience
of trying to share something that was all scattered and you couldn't
quite distill it and verbalize anything worthwhile?   When you
learned it, the content seemed so good, but somehow it didn't come
out as significantly as you had hoped. The reason that happens is
because the cup isn't filled to the point of flowing over. Instead,
we're taking a cup that's not quite full and shaking it in an attempt
to get something to overflow.

Our motivations for "forcing" truth like that may be pride (to
impress others), or the classic attempt to fill those embarrassing
silent moments in the meeting (we'll no doubt need to talk more
about this at some later point). Whatever the reason, our "teaching"
needs to come from the overflow, not from our ambition, our head-
knowledge, or our insecurity about quiet moments in a gathering.

By way of example, it is incredible to me that Jesus was 30
years old before He did anything publicly. Didn't He know His Bible
prior to that? Of course we know from His visit to the Temple at
the age of twelve that He had an incredible understanding even by
that time. Yet it was only to be released in the timing of God
Almighty. "*Today* this is fulfilled in your hearing" (Lk.4:21). It
seems certain that He was no "pew potato" prior to this day, but
Scripture clearly shows that He did not presume the role of being a
"teacher" to others prior to the call and empowering of God when He
was 30 years old. If Jesus didn't take upon Himself, even with His
immense credentials, the position of "teacher" or "shepherd" or
"leader," we had better not either![37]

John the Baptist, in the same way, was 30 years old before he
received "utterance" of the Lord. Was he unqualified to be a
"teacher" of others prior to age 30, by the way we measure
"qualified"? Actually, by "natural" standards, he was very qualified
prior to age 30. He was seemingly a Nazarite, knew his Bible
backwards and forwards, had possibly 15 years in the wilderness to
study the scrolls, and his dad was a priest. No doubt he knew most

---

[37] Hebrews 5:4; Philippians 2:5-8; Romans 10:15.

everything there was to know about the scrolls, the Scriptures. And yet, according to the Bible, he was 30 years old before he received *true* utterance from the Lord (Lk.3:1-2). There was a critical time of preparation. Jesus, John the Baptist, David, Moses, Elijah, Paul, and many others were the same.

Please get this point: Slow down! Don't quickly grab the next neat new thing that comes along and decide to share it with everybody, whether from some platform, in a living room, or at the dinner table. Treasure it in your heart. Take your time. Distill it, digest it, and talk to God about it. Ask Him about it, and just begin to work it through. Let it become part of you. Don't jump at the first chance to spew it out. Wait and watch patiently as you work and pray through it, and wait for *God's* timing to overflow from your heart. Yes, "everyone brings a word of instruction, a song, . . . " and more! Still, we must learn together the meaning of *"from Him and through Him and to Him are all things."* [38] We'll talk more about this as we continue.

Read a few verses with me, and we'll make an application.

(Isaiah 39:1-6)
At that time the king of Babylon sent letters and a present to Hezekiah, for he heard that he had been sick and had recovered. And Hezekiah was pleased with the envoys, and showed them the house of his treasures - the silver and gold, the spices and precious ointment, and all his armory - all that was found among his treasures. There was nothing in his house or in all his dominion that Hezekiah did not show them.
Then Isaiah the prophet went to King Hezekiah, and said to him, "What did these men say, and from where did they come to you?" And Hezekiah said, "They came to me from a far country, from Babylon." And he said, "What have they seen in your house?" So Hezekiah answered, "They have seen all that is in my house; there is nothing among my treasures that I have not shown them."
Then Isaiah said to Hezekiah, "Hear the word of the Lord of hosts: 'Behold, the days are coming when all that is in your house, and

---

[38] Romans 11:36-12:8.

what your fathers have accumulated until this day, shall be carried to Babylon; nothing shall be left,' says the Lord.

(2Chronicles 32:31)
   "However, regarding the ambassadors of the princes of Babylon, whom they sent to him to inquire about the wonder that was done in the land, God withdrew from him, in order to test him, that He might know all that was in his heart."

   The application? Count as precious the "treasures" that our Father gives to you (Mat.16:17; 11:25-27). Please don't be guilty of just dumping from your mouth everything that comes to your conscious mind! God will sometimes "test our hearts" by allowing messengers from Babylon to come to us bearing gifts and flattery. Don't be guilty of carelessly showing off all that is in your heart. Only in God's Wisdom and Timing will anything of lasting value be accomplished anyway (1Cor.3:6; Mk.4:26-29; Jn.15:5-8). At other times He will test our hearts by seeing if, even in the midst of the Saints, we can restrain from drawing attention to ourselves.

   I am *not* suggesting that anyone "bury his talent." I'm simply stating that to say something "Scriptural," or even something "profound" *and* "Scriptural" is not necessarily to speak the "living and active" Word of God. Satan quoted Scripture to Jesus, but that was certainly not God's word to Jesus at that moment of time. Everything that is "Scriptural" is not necessarily the "Word of God," "the very oracles," the "utterance of God" (1Pet.4:11; Jn.15:5; Rom.8:14; Mat.10:20; Lk.3:2) at a particular moment. Jesus *wrote* the Scriptures, yet still never said a single word that He did not hear the Father saying at that moment (Jn.5:19-20, 6:57, 8:28-29, 14:10). As long as you or I are flippantly "horizontal" (simply dealing with "principles" rather than with God Himself) in our approach to Truth, we can never know the meaning of . . .

   "As many as are led by the Spirit are Sons of God,"

   "If any man speaks, let him speak as the very oracles of God,"

   "Christ in you, the hope of Glory,"

   "the full measure of the stature of Christ," and

"So shall My word be that goes forth from My mouth; it shall not return to Me void, but it shall accomplish what I please, and it shall prosper in the thing for which I sent it."

All of this applies (with Jesus as the Standard) regardless of how mature we are, or perceive ourselves to be. How much more should we guard ourselves from "shooting from the hip" when we are still relatively unchanged in practical life by the Truths that we are learning and desiring to teach others?

SHARED IN HUMILITY

If you are currently working through some Truth, and it hasn't "become flesh" in you yet, there is a way of sharing it other than "presuming to be a teacher." As a fellow lamb, still growing in the things that you are about to lay before your family, share the teaching, or chapter, or verse in humility and confession. If it is challenging an area of your life and has convicted and awakened you, then share it without apology, as pure Truth. Yet let the Truth you are discovering and not yet walking in be packaged in an unmistakable humility (rather than teaching "as one having authority"). In this way, you won't come across as hypocritical, or daring to be a teacher of something that has not become part of your life yet. Share it, but do it in a spirit of confession and humility. In other words say "Hey, I've been studying this and reading this and it challenges the dickens out of me. It cuts me to the bone and here's why . . . Here's what I have been doing in my life. Here's the way I have been thinking, and when I read this it made such an enormous impact on me. I want you to pray for me that I'll line up with this." That humble approach is much different than "presuming to teach."

Note that, when sharing your life in this Godly vulnerability and humility, the sharing will not be in weakness and pity. Rather, it will be with conviction and eager anticipation of God directly transfiguring your life (1Thes.1:5; Rom.12:1-2). Don't say "Oh, this is too hard for me; I can't believe I act the way I do and when I read this it made me feel twice as bad." Share not with that attitude of weakness and unbelief, but instead: "Look what God said! Jesus, the Word, became flesh. If that Word would become flesh in me, I'd be more like the Anointed One of God! And that's God's will. I know that *all* the Promises of God are Yes! and Amen! in Jesus. Would you all pray with me about that?" Instead of whining in despair or frustration, we speak (even in failure!) a message of Faith with an anticipation of the life and the power and the spirit of God working in our lives.

SHARED FROM REALITY

Although "not many should presume to be teachers," there will definitely be occasions when God will want you to speak out. Difficult situations can come up that force us to figure out who we are. Sometimes, though we are "nobody," we have a responsibility to God anyway! Let me give you an example.

Have you ever been in a gathering or in a home when all the words and songs fall to the ground (I Samuel 3:19)? They drop to the floor with a thud. Nothing seems to have anything other than "theoretical" significance. Words from a Believer who is truly functioning at that moment as a Vessel of God will be Fire and Light from Heaven that "sets captives Free!" A "Living and Active Word" will always "lay bare the motives and intents of the heart," rather than just saturate the air with pious religious jargon. The words that "fell to the ground" were not the Words of God (though Scripture may have been quoted) because they were not "Alive and Active."

Here's where you come in. If no one has the vision and willingness to take the initiative to *change* that when it occurs, please learn to. Of course, do it in Jesus' way ("full of Grace and Truth"), but stop the big show! If no one responds to your desire and prayers to draw the gathering to a real transaction with Jesus, you may actually even ask in a kind and wise way why everything is so "plastic." When it's a "show" – a little "devo" or "Bible Study" that does not touch Reality, Jesus says to us as He did (through Paul) two thousand years ago, "Your meetings do more harm than good." Expect and thrust forward towards a true Christ-led time together, and don't be afraid to break the hypnotic spell of the religious meeting. For the sake of Jesus, be kind – but don't be mastered by religious protocol and fear of men. "No man can serve two masters."

Possibly it's just our personal fear or lack of any convictions from God that hinder us. Nevertheless, we must have enough courage and honesty to break that barrier and be the People of God in reality. Then if songs start to thud, it's no problem to say:

> "Is everyone alright here? Is Truth reigning in each life, and each marriage? John, how are you and Linda *really* doing since you confessed your selfishness a few evenings ago? Mark, you seem a little "out of it" tonight. What's up? Does anyone else notice a lack of God's Fullness here, or is it just me? (It may be simply my poor discernment, or my lack of touch with God.)"

Realize that we *can* walk together in honesty. We *must.* I am not speaking of a "gripe session." But at the same time I am encouraging the honesty to ask, "Does anyone else notice the problem here?" There will be times where everything is "falling to the ground," and seemingly no lives are being changed "from one degree of Glory to another." If we continue to simply go through the motions, a Gallup poll amongst even the visitors would probably reveal the dominant response to be "Yawn." Contrast that with the visitor "falling on his face and crying out 'God is really here!'"

I'll tell you what brings people to their knees. It is honesty before God and men. "Truth," "Aletheia," "Reality," is the conduit through which God works (John 8:31-32, 8:44, 4:24, 14:6; 1John 1:5-10). With the right heart, you can freely say,

> "I want the Power of God, rather than any mere words (1Cor.4:20) to reign tonight. Is the problem unconfessed sin, or lack of a prayerful life-preparation? Is our ability to drive hard towards the Throne of God waning because everyone is tired? Is the Spirit being grieved by something? Or am I missing the mark in bringing this up? Maybe Jesus is done with us for the evening. Should we call it a night?"

God can work through this honesty to reveal the hearts of men and do His Work. Watch and see. It won't always be "fun," but His Glory is an awesome thing whether it is "fun" or not (Acts 5:9-14).

Often our reason for backing away from dealing truthfully in a gathering is that we may not want visitors there to feel "uncomfortable." In our minds we want to protect the visitors from dirty laundry. We can't allow such a fear to dictate the nature of our gatherings if we truly want to function honestly with one another and with God. In the New Testament church meetings everything was done "for the edification of the *Body*," not for the visitors. As I mentioned earlier, God works through this honesty, through Disciples dealing truthfully with one another in Love, and through the gifts that are unleashed in response to this vulnerability. Whether it's offering the simplicity and beauty of our gifts to Him and each other, nailing carnality in the assembly, bringing teaching from Heaven, Worship and Adoration, or confessing our failures and struggles . . . the unbeliever can see "these people aren't playing games!" Allowing Jesus to touch us and use us in this way lays bare the hearts and motives of the honest visitors. We *must* walk in Truth, in Reality. No religious presentations will ever accomplish God's best Work!

In endeavoring to do God's work in this way, we have definitely now opened ourselves up to the possibility of carnality's reign of terror. For instance, when a church or individuals in the church are still weak, a confession of sin *may* be prompted by carnality. Possibly we confess something designed to vent frustration. Guard against that kind of childishness. Still, it may be legitimate to ask, "Is there unconfessed sin here? What seems to be the problem? Did everybody come with their life in such a state that they could draw near to God?" It may be a very wholesome and freeing thing to lay it on the carpet.

I need to say it again because it is such a difficult thing for so many of us: Please don't be intimidated by visitors. Don't be anxious for their comfort or frightened by their potential judgments. Remember, again, that everything is done for Jesus Himself and "for the edification of the Body" (1Cor.14) – not for the visitor's approval. Our purpose for sharing life together is for Jesus and the body of Christ. If the visitors do see Christ in this way, they're going to be convicted by God's Love and Righteousness. If they see our "love for *one another*" (John 13:34-35), they'll know this thing is from Heaven and not from men. Our job is not to impress them with the things we say, but to show the life of Christ and to allow Him to penetrate their lives or expose their sins. *Beware of performing for visitors.* It is dead wrong. It is manipulation and hypocrisy. We don't need to do that.

All important: be HONEST with what's currently happening.

As foreign as it may sound to the ears of those of us who have grown up being stifled by the traditions of men and unbiblical clergy/laity distinctions, *each* of us do need to be able to touch reality in a gathering. To put it as bluntly as I can, for the sake of the millions of hurting people that "attend services" without finding "power from on High," and for the millions who never will attend services for the same reason, we cannot be slaves any longer to religious exercises. God never intended to meet our needs by pushing them into a counseling office, or by sanctioning an "after-service restaurant evaluation session." Very often He intends to meet our needs through His Church, His "treasure in earthen vessels," His Priesthood "competent to counsel and train one another,"[39] that "the gates of hell cannot prevail against."

It is a responsibility as a Priest of the Most High God to participate as God directs, in harmony, as far as is possible, with the leadership and the moment. In a difficult situation (and some will come up when the stage is removed and replaced with Truth and Life), God may call anyone to ask: "Does anybody have an idea of what might be causing the awkwardness here? It seems that something's out of bounds." Let's all get off the showboat and talk honestly when we're together – about the reality of our lives.

Can you imagine such a thing as a "common" person being able to speak up in your environment? Biblically, anyone has the right – no, the *responsibility* – to do the Work of the Father in a gathering of his Family. In the most difficult of situations you could still ask: "Would it be all right if I asked this blunt question?" If you are

---

[39] Romans 15:14.

genuine, in asking it that way you're still coming from a state of humility, rather than as an expert.

Approach challenging situations that come up carefully, with a quiet heart. If your heart is reactive and your pulse is racing, *wait.* Make sure that you're speaking out of security and strength and peace in your heart (though you wouldn't be human if you weren't a little nervous!), not out of reaction. Do you know what I mean? You have probably felt that pounding heart – hold it, "can" it. You can restrain yourself – "the spirit of the prophet is subject to the prophet." Pray through it and, if necessary, fast through it before you speak out.

We'll talk more about leadership a little later on, but let me say a pertinent word here first. Hopefully you are seeing a distinction being made here. Your place, if you are speaking as a "teacher," must be supported not by religious office, but rather the clear *Life* of Jesus in you – authority in the *unseen* world, as in Acts 19:15. Your life is affirmed amongst God's Elect, and the Shepherd's Voice in you is clear to all (not just your own assessment of yourself, or that of the pigskin, diploma, on the wall). Fullness in Christ is the subject James is promoting when he says that not many should presume to be teachers. As we've seen, that isn't to say that not many should teach. "You ought to teach by now!" said the Hebrews writer to those who were still dull infants long after their conversions to Christ. Everyone should participate in the Priesthood, but usually from a posture of humility, rather than as a "teacher." No one should be less than humble, but the admonition of the Scriptures is this: "not many should presume to be *teachers.*"

To take it a step further for a brief moment, the difference between teaching, sharing a word of instruction or revelation, and BEING an apostle, prophet, evangelist, shepherd, or teacher – is "giftedness," stature, and fruitfulness in the unseen World. There are Gifts, the Scriptures tell us (Ephesians, Chapter 4), that Christ gives to the Church from on High.

Are you are recognized by the fruit of your life (beginning with your wash basin and towel "ministry"[40]) to be walking in a

---

[40] John 13:1-17, 34-35.

high measure of Christ's Giftedness and Stature? If not, you will need to offer your life in more reserve than a tested, approved man or woman might. Rather than speaking as a "teacher," *often* (except in a prophetic moment) it would be far better to say, "Would it be all right if I share this thing?" In that way, you make yourself more vulnerable to someone saying, "No." And you won't get defensive, indignant, or wounded if they do say "no," because you've offered your question in *honest* humility. "The sheep know the Shepherd's Voice." If what you have to say is really from God rather than from ego, God's true People will hear it and *embrace* it. It certainly could not be objectionable to offer a word in humility, laying it before the feet of the Saints, unless one were in it for his own recognition or security.

When the People of God are meeting together it's not a given that it's right for *everyone* to speak (or to remain silent!). Jesus, as the Head, makes the decisions, unless we are disconnected from Him. And I'm not speaking here of a far-fetched "Jesus told me to tell all of you this" sort of charismatic exhibitionism. I am talking about a reasonable, intimate relationship with the Carpenter from Nazareth. And Jesus is very practical, as can be seen in the Gospels, and in the letters from those (like Paul and John) who knew Him well.

Let me give you an example about a *wrong* time to speak out or lead a song. It may sound silly, but believe me, it can happen! There may be times when, right after a purging of sin in a person's life, someone in the Church begins the song "Purify Me." Right then a new Christian may want to sing "Blue Skies and Rainbows." Why would anyone want to sing this song at this touching moment? Possibly because he or she (in their immaturity) had no concept of the importance of what had just happened. They just liked the song. Or, maybe they threw in an upbeat song because they are deathly afraid of a serious moment and want to cheer things up. ". . . After all, Christians are supposed to be joyful." [41]

If someone does respond carnally or shallowly and start such a song, if it truly is not appropriate, someone will have to say, "No,

---

[41] This is, of course, true to an extent, but don't forget that our Messiah was called (prophetically) "a man of sorrows, acquainted with grief."

please don't." That's really not an easy, or common thing to do! Yet, disorder and an illogical sequence of teaching, or prayer, or even praise, is not likely to emanate from the Father. God is not the author of chaos.[42] There's a dynamic, a reasonableness, in the leading of Jesus. Sensitivity to God Himself is necessary. If a person wants to sing "Blue Skies and Rainbows" out of randomness and prayerlessness right after "Purify Me Lord," they *probably* aren't in touch with the Head of the church. Or if someone wants to talk about Grandpa's hangnail immediately after a sober confession, I would want to talk to them about that. That's probably not like Jesus.

Something of that nature really happened at a gathering some time back. Someone, a visitor actually, started talking about their dead cat (and various other side issues again and again) after a few people had opened up their lives in a very sensitive and heart-touching way. And then, there we were, forced to talk about dead cats?! Though I had never met this person, after praying in anguish for a few moments, I passed a note to the one who was showing this insensitivity and asked them to stop doing that, and to simply listen for awhile. I suggested to them briefly in the note that beelzebub (Mat.12:27-28) was, translated, king of the flies, and that the buzz-buzz of interruptions is not like Jesus. In that case, though it was risky (and not warmly received), I was convinced that it was the right thing to say. A few days later, this person who had spoken in such spiritual tones prior to that gathering, was unmasked by a couple of saints that visited them in their home. They then admitted to being a spiritist and proficient in witchcraft – paraphernalia and all. I wish I could give you a happy ending to that account, but I think you at least understand my point.

Shouldn't it be possible for Jesus to expose such demonic things and silence their dominance, as He did while He was here demonstrating His Life for us? Sometimes it will happen in such practical ways as passing such a note during a gathering, but it must happen. Otherwise, satan will see to it that we are slaves to the "beelzebub" interruptions of God's Work in our hearts.

---

[42] 1Cor.14:33.

So again, be sensitive to what's happening. Make yourself vulnerable. While not presuming to be a teacher, still refuse to "bury your talent!" Be willing to stand against that which seems to be harming God's Work, in love, and with courage. It might have grave consequences, as in the case just mentioned, if we back away from our responsibilities.

CONCLUSION

As we discussed earlier, there are two different ways of sharing things. On the one hand, you can share from a "teacher" vantage point - yet God said "not many should presume to be teachers." This "I am teaching you all something" attitude in sharing (what we hope is Truth) in the gathering depends on whether that Word has become flesh, real, *in* you. You are *walking* in it, not hypothesizing based on something you read or heard. On the other hand, if you're still churning and struggling with the Truth of which you are speaking, you can speak it in humility. It would then come out more like: "Hey, I'm not really up to speed on this myself, but I really, really want to be. I can see the importance of this and I want to move hard into it. Anybody else want to join me?" In that way it is shared out of humility rather than out of stature, in a "teaching" mode. The concern you may have is brought out as an honest question, not an accusation. You're asking in the humility of "What seems to be the problem here?" as opposed to being especially bold. That attitude would be a big problem coming from one of unproven fruitfulness and stature. While we allow for the prophetic element coming from even Balaam's donkey, far more often it is Wisdom to share in humility.

I realize that all of this warning about "how to share" could tend to make one paranoid about stepping out and opening up your life. To make things worse, most everyone has had years of practice in passivity in gatherings, as the clergy/laity system has almost completely atrophied 95% of all Christians.

If you'll just take a peek at all that God has given you, you'll have no problem whatsoever with paralysis! You lack nothing except some "equipping" in the use of what God has *already* given you! All the riches of Christ have already been given to you (Eph.1:3). His life and power are already poured out upon us. You *can* make it! Stephen and Paul and Elijah are men "just like us." *God* said that! We need only grow in Faith and Obedience, and go and "possess the land" that God has given us. Certainly it won't be without battles and "giants" in the land. Once we get into that "land flowing with Milk and Honey" – a walk of Life and Power (reread, if you will, footnote #19, page 27) – we'll still feel "like grasshoppers" at times. But the land will be ours. By the Word of the Living God. *"Not by might, not by power, but by my Spirit,"* saith the Lord. When you approach the Word of Truth, do it with a spirit of strength and eager anticipation of what God has done and is doing – because you know the end of the story.

(2Timothy 1:7)
    "For God has not given us a spirit of fear, but of power and of love and of a sound mind."

And the end of this story is, according to the Word of God, nothing less than the "full measure of the stature of Christ." Look it up! If your life terminates on this planet a little earlier than reaching that point (and it will, but that is not an excuse to lower the call of God to something else), so be it. You'll see Him face to face and it'll speed up the process. But the point is this: you know where God is going with your life. He's committed to the task of transforming you, so there is no need to worry. You can go into that land knowing that you're a grasshopper, but also knowing that "He who is in you is greater than he who is in the world."

You don't have to fear the giants in the land because God has already given you that land. He has already given you the potential – living inside of you – of "the full measure of the stature of Christ." Care deeply and, as Paul, "work harder than all the rest," "buffeting your body daily," but don't *worry* about discrepancies between you and the full measure of the Stature of Christ. *Anticipate* and exclaim "Oh, boy! This land is mine! As far as I can SEE." [43]   He

---

[43] Genesis 13:14-18; Joshua 1:3ff.

graciously gives "Life to the Full" **little by little**[44] so that we're not consumed by pride. Surpassing great revelation requires a thorn in the flesh so that we don't become conceited.[45] He gives the Land little by little, or it will eat us up. But know that the land is yours as far as the eye can see – wherever you have the Faith to plant your feet. As much Jesus as you can see belongs to you.

Therefore, don't be afraid or condemned when you share the Word of God in confession and humility. "*Reckon* yourselves dead to sin" and alive to Christ Jesus. "Reckon" in this verse is an accounting term. The books are closed. Count it as done. You are dead to sin, and alive to Christ Jesus. If you'll read Romans 6 and Romans 8 you'll see what power is available for the victory over sin and death. Those things are clearly a matter of possessing the land (if we walk by the Spirit, chapters six and eight, rather than by the law, chapter seven). Even though we're grasshoppers (there's no denying it!), our God is able. There is nothing to worry about. It's our land.

So, having given you much to think about, let me give you another (paradoxical) encouragement which is probably appropriate at this point: Loosen up and have some fun as you explore His Riches! Don't take yourself so seriously![46]

---

[44] Exodus 23:29-30; Deuteronomy 7:22.

[45] 2Corinthians 12:7.

[46] Cassettes available of gatherings where some of this thought was expressed or experienced: Spanky and the Gang Take the Land and Have Fun, and Do Take the Kingdom.

Chapter Eight

Let Jesus
Run The Meeting

I F Jesus is truly the head of the body, the Church, and He is *really* in our midst when we gather in His Name (Mt.18:20), then we had better let *Him* run the meeting. It is imperative that we be responsive to Him, rather than doing some great thing *for* Him, by singing and praying and "preaching." We have a choice of whether to be responsive to the King of Glory Who's in the room, or to run a meeting FOR Him and let Him know the results at the end. The latter is obviously not the way it should be. Don't plan how and when and where you're going to do some great thing in "next week's gathering." Studying Romans 3, praying all night, singing, sharing, . . . these all seem like spiritual things (and might actually be so), yet when they interrupt what Jesus, the Chosen One of God, wants to do, they are rude distractions.

Please! Don't come in with everything all figured out in advance of the meeting. Though at times we may have an idea what His desire may be, Jesus is the *only* One who has the right to decide what we're going to do. (I'm going to say more about that in a minute, so don't get carried away with that point.)

For a good amount of time now, we, in the Church that God has placed my family in, have chosen to meet with Jesus as if He were telling the truth when He said He would be in the room as the Head of the Church. I am not advocating chaos, nor has there been chaos in the time we have yielded His Church back to Him in this way. Certainly you may from time to time know in advance of some teaching or exhortation that is pressing and needs to be brought to Jesus' Church. I am not suggesting that informality, and lack of "considering how we might spur one another on to love and good works," are inherently spiritual. I am saying that we can write Jesus right out of the script with our great ideas, songs, prayers and Bible studies, if we are operating with religious blindness. And I'm determined not to subject Jesus to that anymore if I can help it.

There have been times when I've come prepared to offer something to the Saints (even with xeroxed copies of something in hand) for four months, on probably 70 different occasions, and still have not shared it to this day. Everything must be subject to God's timing, and not our intellect and preparation time. The rationale of the religious world is: "If I put in 40 hours preparing the "sermon," and they're expecting me to preach it on Sunday, I guess I'd better do it, shouldn't I?" Not so in the Kingdom of God, where Jesus runs the meeting. A person can put in his 40 hours (preparing his life, not a "message"), but he shouldn't assume that Jesus wants him to present a "sermon" FOR GOD on Sunday morning. ("Sermons" and "Sunday morning Services" are man-made concepts anyway. At least if the Bible is the Standard that we are using.) That's just not the nature of the Kingdom. Perhaps a teaching may be offered to the saints from a brother in the Family who has spent many hours in prayer and consideration of a particular Truth. God doesn't, however, endorse everything on which we've decided to spend a lot of time.[47]   Your job is to prepare your life, not to prepare "sermons." Prepare your life, not Bible studies. Hide your life in Christ, be filled with the Spirit and He will speak what HE pleases. If we do this, He'll have earthen vessels who can do His Work.

If we allow the Word to become flesh in us, Jesus will be able to do His Work amongst us. He doesn't need our "help." Making plans five years in advance with little calendars of who, how, when, and where we're going to do everything is a direct affront to Jesus'

---

[47] The Bible is full of teaching about the Word of God not simply being something that can be apprehended and grasped by mere intellectual pursuit. Since the Spirit of the Living God authored the Scriptures, it is only (as Jesus and Paul both insisted) by the same Spirit that we can truly apprehend the Truths contained therein. "The man without the Spirit does not accept the things that come from the Spirit of God. They are foolishness to him, and he cannot understand them because they are spiritually discerned." It requires a life that is sanctified wholly to Him. Otherwise, we can aspire to be a great "Bible teacher" and be totally out in left field, as a judgment from God. "Some have wandered away from a pure heart, a good conscience, and an un-faked faith and have wandered away into purposeless words. They are ambitious to be teachers of the Bible, but they have no understanding of the words they use or the subjects about which they make dogmatic assertions" (1Cor.2:11-3:1; 1Tim.1:5-7; 2Thes.2:10-12; Mat.11:25-27). These are statements of God's ability and right to blind the minds of those who do not truly offer their lives to Him, but just try to reach the heights of God by building a Babylonian tower of religious words. It won't work! Give Him your life first!

current Lordship of His church. Can you imagine the Twelve doing that when Jesus was with them? (Generally though, this "script" is out of good intentions, rather than the other possible motivations of fear of failure, or pride and ambition to impress men).

The plans always sound so good. For example, an "all night prayer meeting on Wednesday, the twenty-third" sounds so respectable and spiritual. However, I know that you remember from your earliest knowledge of Jesus, that our Lord taught that if there is any relationship problem we are not *allowed* to pray. Remember? We are to lay our gift down and make that relationship right first. Clearly, prayer may not be what Jesus wants us to do on that particular night. If we are not open to that possibility, we're going to miss a lot over time.

"What could possibly be wrong with regularly starting our meeting with thirty minutes of praise and worship?" some may ask. As one brother from Great Britain said, *starting a meeting with thirty minutes of pre-programmed praise and worship is no different than setting a planned time to kiss your wife.* It's a little shallow, don't you think? At least ask your spouse what he or she would think!

I'd add that worship at a staged, pre-programmed "worship service" **can** be fairly similar to kissing a television set that is projecting an image of a person that you love. The person you would be kissing looks about the same as the real person, and in a sense the kiss would be directed at the real person (not a different person that is a counterfeit), but it would still be far from the genuine article! Similar to pre-programmed worship, it just would not be the same as the spontaneous overflow of life, would it?

Everything must be subject to God's Life and timing, and not our intellect, marketing expertise, flair for drama, or "preparation" time. If we choose to continue robbing the priesthood and man-handling our direction in meetings *to protect ourselves from mistakes, boring times, and coup attempts,* it will be our loss. We will forfeit much opportunity for exploring the true Jubilant, Creative Zoe-Life[48] of the Father.

Lest anyone overreact (as some always do), there is also a right time to plan in advance. At times, such as when facilities must be rented (in certain instances, such as for a park, a campground, a gymnasium, a roller rink, or an auditorium), or tickets to an event purchased, planning in advance is a necessity.

I recall another instance when planning was necessary. I knew that God would have us tie up loose ends in regard to some things that needed to be taught in the church here. We planned to delve deeper into three half-completed topics. As a church we just needed more illumination in these particular areas. I had read a Scripture, "My food is to do the will of Him who sent Me and to *finish* His work" – and I became very convicted that all of the "open issues" that we had begun, such as specific teaching on "satan's devices," were incomplete and needed to be wrapped up. Bread from the Father is to *finish* His work, and sometimes it takes a degree of discipline to do that. And so it was very important to me that some of those loose ends be tied up. That was the first time in ages that anyone wrote up a schedule for the week. At that time, it seemed right and necessary to plan in advance (though it hasn't happened since then). While we were all open to any other direction that our God might want to take us during the week,[49] tying up loose ends was something that we were all pretty certain needed to happen that particular week.

---

[48] "Zoe" is the Greek Word that Jesus used to contrast the kind of life that people have without Him (animal, of-this-world, natural "psuche"-life – the word that we have derived the word "psychology" from) with Life that is truly Life. His Life within those that put their trust in Him. Life that springs from Eternity. Life that existed in God and His Christ before the world was.

(John 10:10-11)
"I came that they might have Life (Zoe), and have it to the full . . . . The Good Shepherd lays down His life (psuche) for the sheep."

There is no mistaking it – **true** Christianity, bought by the blood of the Lamb, is awesome! The very Zoe of God breathed into mere mortals (John 5:24-26, 3:15, 6:35, 6:63; Acts 3:15; Col.3:4; 1Jn.3:14; 2Cor.5:4; 2Tim.1:10).

[49] James 4:13-17; Mat.6:34.

There will be instances that gatherings might be arranged far in advance. Don't rule that out in a legalistic sense any more than you'd lock schedules in systematically. My point is to be open to God. And don't worry – the "communication problem" (calling the entire church together, even on short notice, *even* on a "school night") is not such a big deal as someone might imagine. Particularly not if everyone is "seeking first the Kingdom" rather than trying to squeeze the Kingdom into their own sinfully cluttered lives and priorities. (If the church isn't composed of Christians, **Luke 14:33**, it's not really a Church anyway! Its "Lampstand" has boon removed.)[50]

Jesus wants a People of which He can truly be the "Head" – a "Body" that is as absolutely responsive to Him today, minute-by-minute . . . as His physical body was to His head when He was here on earth in the flesh. No hesitation. No second-guessing!

---

[50] Revelation 2:5.

Chapter Nine

Be A Giver

THIS is a crucial point that I'd like you all to take very, very seriously. Do come, both to the highways and byways and to the gatherings of His Saints, prepared in your heart to be a giver. You know by now that I am *not* referring to being a spiritual hero and regurgitating something that you've studied up on in a commentary, or read in a book, or heard on a cassette tape. Let the Word of God read you on a continual basis. Let it "make its home in you richly." Prepare your heart. And then you'll be able to consider, ponder, question, and think in advance as to how you might "spur one another on toward love and good deeds" (Hebrews 10:24-25). (This verse in Hebrews is in the context of "don't get in the habit of not gathering together as His People," vs. 25.) Consider what the Holy Spirit is doing in you. Don't come as a spiritual vegetable, ready only to receive.

You're not at the gathering to watch a show and soak in your fill, right?! (Did you know that you can even be guilty of having a dry "worship service" in miniature even in a living room!) That attitude of "feed me" is similar to the role of babies in a household. They only take and take and cry, and never contribute. In other words, please don't assume the "baby's" role, but rather take responsibility in God's Household. Hear that again, underline it and add an exclamation point. PLEASE take responsibility for your life, and the lives of others. I cannot emphasize that enough. Nobody's going to do it for you. Be a giver, look for others' needs, and live to meet them as Jesus did.

Come prepared. That will require that you live the Life outside of meetings, not just at meeting time. If your life is hidden in Christ and you're busy delving into the deep things of God and the hearts of men, rather than wasting time on trivia, junky entertainment and hobbies, you will naturally burst with the life of Christ during meetings. You won't be tempted to "crank" something out. If you are living with all of your heart, soul, mind and strength for the Kingdom of God, your life will be buried in God's things. It won't, in that case, be a problem to come prepared or have something to offer your brothers and sisters. You won't have to grunt and groan to get something out, or scurry off to the latest book and see what you had underlined so you can bring something. It's not that way at all. If your life is hidden in Christ always, and not just theoretically in meetings, His overflow will pour out of you. And it will be as likely to happen in a living room at ten minutes after five or a quarter till seven as it is at an 8:30 gathering.

If it is not our LIFE before God and if we are not really "joined and knit together" with our brothers and sisters on a seven-day-per-week basis, then I perceive we have the wrong idea about what gatherings are for!

Purify Me

If I should die tomorrow
And this face you'd never see again,
There's one thing I beg, my friend:
That's never give up.

Keep on singing . . .

Purify me Lord from ways that aren't of you,
Take away the old and make my life brand new.
I surrender all to you – not my will but Thine.
The sweetest thing I know is letting your Love show.

Through the trials and heartaches
Remember why He came, my friend.
You know the Light shines to the end,
So never give up.

Keep on praying . . .

Purify my heart, I yield to you each part
Help me to run into your arms when the purifying starts
I surrender all to you – not my will but Thine
The less there is of me, the more of You I see.

Make yourself as nothing   (Mat.10:32-39; Phil.2:3-16; Heb.11:6),
No "feelings," no rights, my friend.
You'll be rewarded in the end,
So never give up.

Melody, Cindy

Chapter Ten

Meetings:
A Means, Not An End

MEETINGS are not the pinnacle of Christian service. If we are not living it in our homes, with our families and roommates, and taking it to the streets and jobs . . . then our meetings, no matter how formal or how "free," will be a dangerous farce. The "excellent meetings" will be a very deceitful substitute for a corporate Christ-life that truly celebrates Jesus together in Life, as well as in meetings. It's extremely misleading to say or act like "meetings" are what Christianity is all about (even when filled with lively praise). This is deceiving because it seems "so spiritual" to sing songs and to pray and to hear powerful teaching from the Word of God. However, a glimpse into the Life of Jesus, and the record of His Church, can only lead us to the conclusion that "spiritual" meetings are not the essence of Christianity. Those times together will only be wasted (in God's sight – Isa.1:10-20) if we aren't abiding in Christ with our families, on the job, and in the shopping malls. What's the point of singing songs together before a meal, when the whole church is together on Saturday or Sunday afternoon, if it would never cross our minds to sing at home, or when people are visiting?

Note the way we subconsciously categorize our lives. Rip out the religious exercises no matter how "neat" they seem to be; they are only litter, unless the undergirding of the whole thing is life. Our goal is not to establish a new "informal" tradition. On the contrary, the idea is that our meetings be undergirded by our lives being hidden in Christ – a celebration and overflow of real life. Whether everyone participates by bringing a word of instruction, revelation or hymn, or whether we have two songs, a prayer and a paid Bible class teacher to deliver a lesson – regardless of which end of the spectrum we're on, no one could disagree that the meeting will be wasted if our lives aren't committed to being buried in Jesus 24-hours-a-day.

The Kingdom of God is neither here nor there, it's within you. "The time will come when you'll neither worship me in Jerusalem or on this mountain." It's not meetings that Jesus is after. *"The Kingdom of God consists not of mere talk, but power"* (1 Cor.4:20). It is imperative that our meetings flow out of the fellowship of living for and in Jesus together, not a routine of scheduled services. Our gatherings MUST be the overflow of our life in Jesus together. What we bring to our God and our Family in Christ at a gathering is a *real* relationship with Christ Jesus Himself, and the overflow of the treasures in the storehouse of your heart.

The only real contribution any of us can make is *who we are*, not an external contribution to make a meeting better. Do you sing to Jesus, as to a living person, face to face, in your *private* time with Him? If not, of what value is it to be swept up in religious "group dynamics" to sing to Him in a meeting? I know that you see what I mean. Work this deeply into your life, brothers and sisters. Work *Him* deeply into your life, and the meetings will take care of themselves. Let's keep pushing on together in life continuously lived for, and in, Christ.

Chapter Eleven

The Dreaded
"P of I"

P LEASE, for the sake of the Testimony of the Son and the peace of all of His Family, please! no pooling of ignorance. That is, don't allow the scenario in which everyone just throws their wisdom, thoughts, experiences, observations, and Bible verses onto the heap. It may sound something like this: "I think that faith is ____." Or, "Well, I went to a church one time where we . . . "; or "I remember when . . . "; or "The International Interdenominational Commentary says that this verse means. . . "; "In the original Aramaic the meaning is . . . ." That kind of thinking could easily be, and usually is, spouting off without communion with God. Or living in the past and "leaning upon our own understanding" because of pride or shallowness. When a certain topic of our interest may arise, we may throw in our so-called wisdom and observations, thinking that we can top the last bit of information that was given. That's not what the Kingdom of God is all about. Don't yield to the temptation to deal in externals in order to keep the conversation going, or to impress others. If our interaction in a meeting doesn't seem to be snapping right along, the carnal man inside each of us is desperate to spice things up and make the meeting dynamic. When we yield to this temptation, we grieve the Spirit by usurping Jesus' Headship. And if everyone's life is brimming with Jesus, that carnal response will never happen – it won't be necessary.

Obviously, meetings in which Jesus is reigning will not be boring or like a traffic jam of unnecessary "spiritual" words. Imagine Paul showing up in Troas and not being able to get a Word in edgewise because everyone had an opinion – but few had an "open Heaven" and a Word from "Home" (Eph.2:6; Col.3:1-3; Jn.17:3; Heb.10:19-20).

Our goal is **not** to get more people to "participate." Our heart is to get more of Jesus into our lives, and the lives of our brothers and sisters. Then the "paticipating" will come from the overflow of God's Heart . . . through us. We'll function out of the current Life of God and the fellowship in the Holy Spirit! That's what it's all about. And so it is with singing as well . . . .

Chapter Twelve

No Sing-Alongs!

D ON'T ask to sing your "favorite" song, but request or initiate the song that best reflects or describes the current condition of your heart, or the current atmosphere or teaching of the gathering. Song is generally prayer – and no one would dream of praying for nice weather for a fishing trip after someone has asked for prayers about a temptation to commit murder. Surely that kind of insensitivity would be obvious. But you understand the point: don't change the subject on God unless there's good reason. Do you see what I mean? Since song is prayer or teaching, don't jump to different subjects because you happen to like a different song. That's not a meeting that Jesus is running.

God is not a God of disorder (1Cor.14:33). What He does, flows. You don't see natural rivers breaking up and jumping all over the place; they flow and have a direction and purpose. In the same way, when God is running the meeting, you'll find that it flows and it's not our place to randomly shotgun all over the place by having a "sing-along."

God does not author or visit sing-alongs. He wants to change and build our lives and our hearts, and the hearts of the people around us. So, as I mentioned earlier, you wouldn't dream of praying for a fishing trip if somebody was confessing rape or murder. That would seem rude and disgracefully insensitive, wouldn't it? Again, the same usually holds true for singing "Blue Skies and Rainbows" right after "Purify Me Lord." You've got to go where God is going. Don't just jump into something the carnal man wants to do next and change the subject on God unless there is good reason. In short, be sensitive to what's happening in the invisible world around each individual in the meeting, as a whole.

If your heart is not bursting to overflow, flash-flood level, then you have two choices. Either ask to sing a song that is a purposeful statement about how you *want* your heart to be before God and man, or just watch and pray and join your heart to what others are initiating. But don't take it upon yourself to initiate. Don't pretend or get religious! To make it simple, "choosing songs" (as with any gift that we offer) must come from a current purpose of a fruitful mind towards God Himself – not a "tune" you are infatuated by or preoccupied with.[51]

Here is another point which ought to be obvious, yet I've seen this absurd carnality even in India. Please don't look up the next song you'd like to sing while we're still singing another song, except in the rarest of cases. That is really bad. It's as bad as reading Mary Poppins during the proclamation of the Oracles of God, or writing notes during a prayer. If you are really singing to the King of Glory, your mind will be on HIM, not the song that *you* want to sing next. God is alive, and desires to be treated as such. Amen.

---

[51] If you find that you could be exhilarated by the melody or the beat, even if the words of the song were to elude you, there is a good chance that it is not truly worship that you are experiencing. At least it would be very important for you to be devoted to keeping your mind fruitful towards God if you are easily moved by the externals of melody or rhythm.

Chapter Thirteen

Corporate Prayer

P RAY in public gatherings if there is a prayer on your heart, *not* because:

A) It's your turn in a "chain prayer";

B) Someone assigned you an opening or closing prayer.

To do such a thing as assigning someone several days or weeks in advance to be the official "prayer-person" (or "sermon-giver," for that matter) is poor, poor, poor! Who can know several weeks or days or even hours in advance who will be functioning in purity and faith and sincerity, and who is therefore even *able* to speak on others' behalf before the Throne of God? Who even knows in advance that a "prayer" or "sermon" is what God desires to happen on the occasion in question?!

C) You want to get in your two bits so no one wonders if you're spiritual.

Can anyone relate to that? You don't want anybody to ask how you're doing, so every once in a while, you pray or say something. Right? That way, no one will wonder if you're doing okay. Please don't do that.

D) You want to pray to fill the gaps so that you or God aren't embarrassed by the lull in the action.

If the prayer's welling up on your heart in reality, pray. If not, don't. Or if you are deliberately and forcefully moving towards God, pray in spite of not being filled to the brim at that moment. Also, please get rid of the religious prayer cliches (protestant and catholic mantras) that so easily roll off our lips when we are lazy, empty, or fear men's opinions! God doesn't like 'em.

Chapter Fourteen

Ritual? No.

T HERE should be, realistically, no more ritual and continued predictability than Jesus exhibited in the three-and-a-half years with his twelve disciples. He had no weekly "Bible Studies" with the men that He was pouring out His Life for. No monthly prayer breakfasts. Jesus began a "religion" that, when lived out in the way that He walked, continues to confound the world. Unlike the other world religions, it is without ritualistic "services," religious incantations, or locked-in form.

If you study church and world history, you'll find that man is a predictable animal who loves ritual. All the world religions of men are filled with ritual for people to hang their hats on. The similarities between religions in that respect is not a coincidence, but part of unregenerate man's fallen religious nature. In other words, fearful, lazy, compromising (and even sincere) religious folks in every world religion (including Americans) may *need* a liturgy, ritual, a legal code and man-made "order" that they attribute to God – to enable them to *know* that they are appeasing god.[52] A Muslim in Cairo told a couple of brothers and myself that their "Mosque Services" consisted of some prayers, some songs, a collection, and a man giving a sermon. He sheepishly confessed that he and many others often dozed off during the speech part. Sound familiar?

Jesus didn't have liturgy. He had very few "things" that you could point to and say "this is the way we do it." He simply lived out his three-and-a-half years with his disciples, walking along the streets and talking with them. He would say, as He spotted an illustration of what He wanted to communicate to them: "The

---

[52] So subtle is this pagan trait of fear and pride in christendom that no one thinks it odd to find, as I did very recently, <u>Roberts Rules of Order</u> displayed prominently on an easel at a Christian Bookstore – right between <u>Smith's Bible Dictionary</u> and <u>Vine's Expository Dictionary of New Testament Words</u>. Most people don't even realize that this textbook on "What is 'Decent and In Order'" is frequently the standard of today's acceptable religion, rather than the Bible.

Kingdom of God is like this field. . ." or "The Kingdom of God is like
a pearl merchant. . . ." In simplicity, they shared their lives in the
Truth and Light of God, roasted hot dogs, laughed, threw a frisbee,
and just plain lived life, out loud and on purpose, together. That
was, and is, the Kingdom of God, with Jesus as the Head.

The early church was not ritualistic. It had no "locked-in"
format. But note this: it was not a "loosey-goosey," "we're too
spiritual to get together," "my church is wherever I am" kind of
universalism. I am not promoting a Sunday morning stay-home-
and-read-the-paper type of pseudo-Christianity. No way! God's
manifested "Holy Nation" will bring about *more* gathering, life-
transferring, transforming, and teaching than ever. In *one day* in the
first century the new Christians encountering Jesus on Pentecost
changed their approach to religion *RADICALLY.* They went from a
religion of "hearing another wonderful message from the Word"
during a Jewish "worship service" at a set time and place[53] to:
"**Every day** they continued to meet together in the temple courts
[city park]. They broke bread in their homes and ate together with
glad and sincere hearts." *This* is Christ's effect on any life swallowed
by His Spirit!   Holiness.   Self-sacrifice.   Depth of relationship.
Everyone.   Lives "joined and knit together by every supporting
ligament."   "And **all** those who believed were together, and had all
things common." Cultural? No way! Read His teaching and watch
His Life. That's just Jesus!

Has your life, and the life of your church, been enveloped by
the Spirit Who was in Jesus? Really? Verifiably? For Jesus' sake,
for His honor and testimony, let's get on our knees and call out to
God for a transformation of the magnitude encountered on Christ's
Pentecost. Settle for nothing less!

Let's go back, for the sake of a somewhat humorous
illustration, to the beginning of Immanuel's ("God with us") life on
earth. In Matthew, chapter two, and Luke, chapter two, we find the
accounts of the shepherds and the wise men coming "to worship"
Jesus, just like we do today. Did it go something like this?

---

[53] Acts 13:27; John 4:21.

"Brother Shepherd Number One will have the opening prayer, Brother Magi Number One will bring us another wonderful message from the Word, Brother Magi Number Two will be taking up the collection, Brother Shepherd Number Two will be leading us in our Song Service today, ... Now, let's all stand for thirty minutes of praise and worship and then we'll . . . ."

It just wasn't that way, was it?! Do you think that's what it meant (or means) to "worship Jesus?" Or was it far more real and natural than that? If that is not what it meant to worship Jesus then, that is not what it means today, either. If that is not what the disciples of Jesus did *then*, with Jesus in their midst (and it definitely wasn't, as the Biblical record shows), then that is not what His disciples need to be doing today, with Jesus in our midst. Especially since He is no longer a child in a manger, but a grown up King, a Wonderful Counselor, Mighty God, Everlasting Father, the Prince of Peace. Other religions go through a set of prescribed rituals on a preset schedule of days and hours for a dead or distant god. But that was never the way of our Teacher, nor the Church that He died for, at least in the early days. Of course, history shows, that it was only a short amount of time before Christianity sagged into the lifestyles and religious practices of its pagan neighbors. But to all who care and long for a better future I say confidently, "It was not so from the beginning."

In the early days of Christianity, the people still viewed themselves as Jews and went to the temple at 3:00 to pray. But as you look through the book of Acts, you'll find less and less of that. By the time of Acts 15, there was a judgment from the elders of Jerusalem to eliminate the requirements of the Law, with exception of the exhortation to continue to not eat blood. And after they broke away from circumcision, they moved farther and farther away from the Jewish legalities and rituals as they realized that these external things that they had held to were only "shadows of the reality that is in Christ" (see again Col.2:16-17; Hebrews chapter 4, 8, 9, 10). They desired to make concessions at times, but the pattern was that these concessions with Judaism and its system, other than the debt of love to the individuals involved, quenched the Spirit and brought only more difficulty.[54]

God has made it clear in His Son. Jesus was and is the spiritual flute playing[55] Alpha and Omega of all the Father's intentions and pleasure. Jesus has made Himself plain by how He lived His Life in the midst of the orthodox religion of His day, and by His teaching. He desires captives set free, not main-streamed and institutionalized in a "service-attending" spiritual orphanage. As an older brother, Tom Holland, has often said, "Let's not 'hold meetings' – let's let them go!" Let's embrace that freedom!

We can easily stifle the Holy Spirit by slumping into ritual or predictability (usually as a security blanket to protect us from the "bogey men" of boring meetings or someone taking over the meeting). Think about it again. If the twelve had felt the need to have an "order of worship" every time *they* met with Jesus, they would have been usurping Jesus' right to run the meeting, would they not? It is no different today. How many ways are there to say it? Jesus is as alive today as He was then, and still deserves to be Head of the Church! As radical, and by now redundant, as it may sound, ungodly clergy/laity systems and ritualistic, decided-in-advance choreography for the "service" have all but destroyed the rights and responsibilities of the Priesthood of Believers, and the Lordship of Christ, in gatherings.

As I've said, there is nothing inherently spiritual about, and there is no special prize for creativity or informality. There is, however, a mandatory need to be led by God, not a calendar, a program, a liturgy, or a hierarchy.

"As many as are led by the Spirit are sons of God."

As a church, we must be free to gather the Saints in the park on a Saturday or Sunday or Monday or Tuesday night – in living rooms, apartment clubhouses, hotel banquet halls, gymnasiums, warehouses, restaurants, city streets (or even a religiously-purposed

---

[54] Acts 18:5-7, 19:8-10, 21:17-30; Galatians 2:11-21, 4:9-11, 5:1-12.

[55] Matthew 11:17-19.

building).[56] Or, as a church, maybe we'll go in smaller numbers to different assemblies during their "service" times and gather together afterwards to pray for the groups and people that we've met. Or possibly God would send every last member of the church, with very little notice, into other nations. We are called to be the people of God who worship "neither in Jerusalem or on that mountain," "neither here nor there." We're free to be and to do. We have no ball and chain that has us trapped in a format by which we must abide. Jesus walked as a friend along the way with his disciples for three-and-a-half years, "daily in public and from house to house," and I'd encourage all of us to do the same with Him, and one another, by living Life out corporately in simplicity and freedom.

I must add here that some whom George Gallop has included as Christians do not yet belong to Jesus Christ – because their faith is not yet in Him. These are not converted to Jesus Christ with "all of their heart, all of their soul, all of their mind, and all of their strength." Some, though "religious, church-going people," will despise

---

[56] Is it not odd that there were no "church buildings" for about the first 250 years of Jesus' Church (<u>Early Christians Speak</u>, Everett Ferguson, p.76; <u>Acts of Paul</u> (2nd Century); <u>Acts of Justin 2</u>; <u>Early Christian and Byzantine Architecture</u>, Richard Krautheimer, pp.1-15; etc.)? This is longer than the United States has currently been a country! That's how long Christianity existed without "church buildings." This is the case even though all of the Jews and all of the pagans that were the new converts had grown up with synagogue and "temple worship" in buildings, at a regularly scheduled time and place. Remarkable. A normal home, acquired and remodeled to hold more people, has been excavated in Dura Europas. This is the "earliest identified christian meeting house" – a structure, though still just a normal abode, specifically for christian meetings (rather than just meeting in homes and "rented halls" and such when the numbers were too large for a home). This "earliest identified christian meeting house" was a "third century" structure!

By just a few decades after Pentecost, the Believers, during a famine of true God-Sent Leadership, were already fossilizing and losing connection with the Head (as evidenced by the compromise and ritualism that had sprung up so quickly – Rev.1-2; <u>Didache</u>; <u>Hermas</u>; <u>II Clement</u>; <u>Epistle to the Philippians,</u> Polycarp; <u>Letter to the Corinthians</u>, Clement of Rome; etc.). In spite of many evidences of spiritual dullness so early on, still they did not revert to the appearance of pagan temple worship with Christian lyrics. Is there a reason why Jesus and the Apostles He had equipped, and the generations that followed, did not follow in the footsteps of the "practical" pagan religions? Of course! Once again, the "religion" the carpenter from Nazareth began was not even remotely similar to those "of this world." Nor can it be today, and still find His highest Blessing and Anointing.

the idea of not having "set times and places." It will bother them no
end that their 20th-Century American idols of lifestyle, job,
vacations, sports, education, "private time" (usually meaning "TV
time") are threatened by their Lord (if He be that to them) possibly
calling on them at any time.

Jesus called out to a man along the way, *"Come with
me."*

"Wait Jesus. Can't you see that I'm mending my nets?
This is important! This is my dad's boat and I do need
to 'honor my father and mother,' don't I? Can't we
make an appointment for, say, every Sunday morning
for a couple of hours? Anything that you have to say
can surely be said in that amount of time."

Then He said to another, *"Follow Me."*

But he answered, "Lord, let me first go and bury my
father."

Jesus said to him, *"Let the dead bury their own dead, but
you go and preach the kingdom of God."*

And another also said, "Lord, I will follow You, but let
me first go and bid farewell to my family."

But Jesus said to him, *"No one, having put his hand to
the plow, and looking back, is fit for the kingdom of
God."*

"That's a little radical and unreasonable, Jesus. I used
to think that way too . . . before I came to understand
the love of God and my position in Christ. My God
would never say such a thing as what you just said!
You don't even seem to understand my situation. I
have two kids and, you know, if a man doesn't get
braces for his kids and save for their college and get
them into after-school activities, he's worse than an

infidel.[57] But after I get these other obligations out
of the way in a few years, I can go on a mission trip for
you, or something like that. I do give 10% (before
taxes!). And I think that you should watch out – you're
beginning to sound (don't get me wrong, I'm not trying
to criticize, but) . . . you're beginning to sound a little
judgmental, legalistic and even cultic . . . ."

*"Do not think that I came to bring peace on earth. I did
not come to bring peace but a sword. For I have come to
set a man against his father, a daughter against her
mother, and a daughter-in-law against her mother-in-law.
And a man's foes will be those of his own household. He
who loves father or mother more than Me is not worthy of
Me. And he who loves son or daughter more than Me is
not worthy of Me. And he who does not take his cross
and follow after Me is not worthy of Me. He who finds his
life will lose it, and he who loses his life for My sake will
find it . . . Depart from me. Though you would have
sworn your allegiance to me on a stack of Bibles, I never
knew you."*

It is frightening how many millions of church-goers have been
deceived by religion because they signed a little card, said a few
words into the air, or got wet. Many (and some, from God's
perspective, who are reading this now . . . stop and at least pray
through it) consider themselves Christians when the teachings of
Jesus and a hundred other Testimonies in the Bible positively deny
the possibility. A person without Life from Heaven, born in death
to self, cannot truly be saved. And if not saved, then obviously not
a part of His Church. And if not a part of His Church, then *no
wonder* they wouldn't want to be where He is, in His Presence and
exposing Light in a gathering, or daily and deeply in the lives of

---

[57] Believe me, I don't say these things lightly. It breaks my heart when anyone
has given up (at least to the naked eye) the means of giving such gifts to their
children. But we must, like the father of our faith, desire to reason "that God can
raise the dead." We will, at the very least, by the Grace of God, offer to our children
"better and lasting possessions." May God strengthen and en-courage us.

others! Regularly scheduled ceremonies and Bible discussions are far safer and more convenient.

To modify a quotation from Samuel Johnson, from the late 1700's, "Ritual is the last refuge of the scoundrel." Why? Because if we can hide behind meeting a minimum requirement of religious "times and places" in order to feel justified before God and man, then we can live any way we please the rest of the time. At least our "socially acceptable" sins (wickedness) will be out of reach. We can live comfortably in the world of "At least I don't _____."

> "You're just judging me! Get the log out of your own eye! Grace covers – we're only human, you know!"

Attending "services" (protestant mass or catholic mass), "waiting on the Lord's Table," preaching sermons, giving to the poor, praying long prayers, speaking in tongues of men or angels, memorizing the Bible, or even lifting hands during worship . . . mean nothing in themselves. I know that you know that in your heart.

Jesus calls out to us in our hazy state:

> *"If you will lay it all down for me, in a statement of absolute trust, all the Heavens and the earth can not contain the gifts and reality from My Life that I will shower upon you. Try me!"*

> *"However, unless I can have all of you: your tongue, your emotions, your savings account, your favorite things, absolute control of your relationships, all of your time (including your all-american family vacation, your 'family time,' your wasted time with TV, etc., your evenings, and even your Saturdays) . . . unless you will turn to me and offer all that you are and could be to me, then you're only fooling yourself. 'Unless you forsake all, you cannot be My follower.'"*

Now we can see why unconverted religious people squawk and cry "Foul! Cult!" when they are challenged to consider the Church of the Bible, rather than the accommodating, luke-warm substitutes of today. "Ritual is the last refuge of the scoundrel."

(Mark 7:7-13)
And Jesus said, "In vain they worship Me, teaching as doctrines the commandments of men. For laying aside the commandment of God, you hold the tradition of men . . . ." And He said to them, "All too well you reject the commandment of God, that you may keep your tradition . . . making the Word of God of no effect through your tradition which you have handed down. And many such things you do."

Please consider the quality of your heart before God, with all issues resolved before the Holy Spirit of God. Then you will have no problem "seeking *first* the Kingdom." Jesus, His House, and His Purposes will be the air that you breathe. You'll be more than anxious to be where Jesus is, where folks are "gathered in His Name." You will grow faster spiritually than you ever dreamed possible, while in the religious world only a tiny, tiny proportion of the "church" population grows beyond the barest infancy (by Biblical standards). Give your whole life to Jesus, destroy the security blanket of ritual, program, and clergy/laity hierarchy (that "make null and void the Word of God") and WATCH! It is wonderful!

If, by some slim chance, you are trembling in your heart as you read this book and its challenges . . . ? If you desire to be all that God wants you to be, but you've failed – if your flesh is weak, if your conscience is fouled by shadows and condemnation, if your hope is blurred . . . ? If any of this is true, **know this:** *God is faithful.* In Christ, no mountain is immovable. None. Biblical history, and all of history since, is filled with men and women just like you and me who have been stripped, by their own foolish sin, of any grounds whatsoever for reliance on their good performance. Murder, immorality, prostitution, lying, unbelief, and every form of darkness imaginable have been cancerous boils on the flesh of so many of the men and women that God has healed, and loved on, and even used in His Plan. They have, of necessity, cast themselves wholly on the mercy of a loving God. Period. That's all that was left. Yet it is enough – and infinitely more. Those that turned to the Lord in their distress, God vindicated by their Faith in the Blood of His Beloved Son. No matter what they have done, regardless of the magnitude of their failings, my failings (and they are shameful), or your failings, **those that call on the Name of the Lord shall never be put to shame.** Pardon me for sounding just a little religious . . . but too bad: Hallelujah!

A Personal "Genesis"

This is now my testimony
To you I long to tell
So good, so rich, so pure, so true,
I have to break the shell.

Before I seemed so happy,
Striving for it all,
The corporate climb and just-in-time,
Everything on the ball.

But in my room, left to myself
And reaching down inside,
I suffered what I clearly knew,
A case of selfish pride.

Too proud to admit
Through all of the gloss
How lonely I was,
How empty and lost.

Where should I go?
To whom would I turn?
No more answers that asked questions,
I had something to learn . . .

In His patient mercy
He began to draw me near.
The Truth's not far,
The door's ajar,
Stand back, it's coming clear.

A Stone that makes men stumble –
It's so easy to be lost.
My home, my job, my friends, my life
Could this be the cost?

. . . Nothing before Him,
everything after . . .
Behold! I see!
The Truth is coming faster!

I praise the Lord in Heaven
Who gave me Faith and Sight.
I bowed my knee to Jesus –
The Truth, the Way, the Light.

No more fruitless goals and dreams,
No more wondering why,
No more empty possessions,
No more living a lie.

God has truly blessed me,
Showed me His Holy Way.
I give my life to Jesus, His Son,
Each and every day!

Sarah
(a new Christian)

Chapter Fifteen

Goo-Goo Spirituality

N OW that you've decided to bow your knee fully to Christ Jesus, don't get weird and super-spiritual, okay? The kind of consecration to God's Purposes that I'm speaking of is not weird at all. It is not clerical or stone-faced. It is not lofty and "cloud nine-ish." That means, commitment to Jesus lived out will *not* result in gushy, romantic, broken-voiced discourses or lofty, ozone spirituality.

Hebrews 4:12-13 speaks of the Living Word of God exposing what we'll call "soulishness." Soulishness is a different animal than true spirituality, though it apes spirituality very well. It looks so wonderful, goo-goo eyes and all. It has an appearance of spirituality, but there's something wrong with it. It will turn your stomach if you're really in touch with God. Fortunately, when the Word of God, the Sword of the Spirit, the Rhema of God, comes forth from the Priesthood of Believers, it divides between soul and spirit; it separates soulishness from spirituality.

It's good to be aware of the nature of soulishness so that we don't fall into it. Spirituality is real. Jesus was spiritual (obviously to the fullest extent possible or imaginable), yet He was a man's man. He was strong. He laughed, He cried. When He was thirsty he said, "I thirst." He didn't say "Praise God, Glory, Hallelujah," every other sentence. Neither did the apostles say "Praise God" with every breath. "Hey, John, let's go to Caesarea, Praise God!" "What do you think about that, James?" "Well, Praise the Lord, Hallelujah!" They didn't act that way. They were real guys who lived it out on real turf. They did not prance around with religious lingo. Their lives were so much deeper than that. You don't see that stuff in any of the prophets, or Apostles, or the Lord's brothers, or Jesus Himself – the true Standard. What you do see when you look at the men that God has accredited is real humanity – "partaking of the Divine nature," in strength and stature. These men, and our Lord, could walk into a crowd of tax collectors without fear, and actually draw them into the Father's Presence.

Let me explain further. If a holy-roller, super-spiritual person with goo-goo eyes went to a party where people were smoking pot, he would be thrown out in a second. Jesus, on the other hand, though He never compromised with sin, was the guest of honor with such people. He was real, He was strong, He was spiritual, but He wasn't "hyper-spiritual." I don't know how else to describe it. He didn't shout, "Glory, Hallelujah." Instead He would say, "Hey, come here a minute, I want to talk to you." He was real, and He was strong.

I hope that gives you a glimpse of the difference between what could be soulish and what might instead be of Christ's Spirit. True spirituality isn't an external, nor does it come with a certain vocabulary. Soulishness does come with these, and more: a certain way to dress, to talk, to act.

You be real, okay?! Find your security in your relationship with the King of Glory, and ignore the pressures of conformity or fear of mere men's opinions. He'll take excellent care of you, and likely gather around you more and more saints who also seek Him with a pure heart.

Chapter Sixteen

A Heart For The Battle

I F you are ever to see True Life expressed on the streets and in the gatherings of God's People, you will have to pay a price to see it. As our Commander once said,

"The Kingdom is entered forcefully, and the violent take it by force."

Whether the "battle" is attempting to bring Life and Integrity to a religious system, or desiring to bring Saints already on that road to higher ground – in either case, it takes energy ("energeo") to see it through! In one case we are trying to find the "liberty of the Spirit," and in the other case we are trying to keep that Life from waning in our midst when things are getting out of line. In either case, we must "take it by force." It doesn't just happen.

Be strong and be overcomers, not survivors or victims. Let the attitude of the victorious Ancient of Days Life within each of you be evident at whatever gatherings that you have. Let me emphasize this point again. Whether during meals together, or in others' homes, or in small or large gatherings, spontaneous or planned, live in reality, expressing the Life within you. There's no way we should be talking about the deep things of God in meetings if the life of Christ isn't exchanged during meals together, with two, five, or ten people. If we are walking in reality and our lives are intermingled, then why would we wait until a whole-church gathering to be "spiritual?" If we wait until the meeting to be "spiritual," it's not spiritual at all. More likely we are driven by something other than Christ. Since true spirituality crosses all time and circumstance lines, you should be just as likely to have a dynamic, heart-rending conversation out of Leviticus 23 after dinner ("off the cuff") as you are at a meeting . . . if it's the real thing. Watch, and take a reading every once in a while. Check the pulse of private times together. Whether two, four, six, sixty-two, or six thousand people are together, small talk won't mark the bulk of the conversation if we belong to God in Truth. Don't "crank out" spirituality because you are "supposed to," but simply live your life in Christ and you'll be naturally consumed with the things of God in or out of a meeting. And when a gathering does come up, you won't have to cross any lines and "put on" a spiritual mind-set. Understand?

What should you do when you are not in the "ideal situation" in the church that you are a part of currently?

Hide your own life in Christ. Spend time with other people who have hidden their lives in Christ. Search out "equipping for the works of ministry" from those who are obviously born of the Wind and Authority of Heaven, and the Lamb.[58]

Draw others one by one into that circle. It won't happen by wishing it were so. Draw yourself to the people who emanate the heart of Christ. Bring people to Christ Jesus and a reality of relationship with Him one by one, and that circle will expand. God will begin to knit your life together with others who care.

If you are "attending" a religious organization that has very little in common with the Church of the Bible, you have, no doubt, been shuddering with trepidation as you have tried to envision all of the above in your environment. Don't run from the situation you're in just yet! Learn the way of the Cross first. Let it be said of you, as your Lord was able to say, "I did nothing in secret." Don't slip out the back door with complaints in your heart. Be able to say, honestly, "I would have gathered you as a hen gathers her chicks, but *you* would not." Be honest. Be open. Be considerate. But don't think that that means you'll need to spend the next 100 years subjecting yourself and your family to a "form of godliness that denies the power." God said clearly how to respond to religious form that is not from Him: "And from such people turn away!" This being true, still very few have ever truly laid down their lives for others – giving all to make a difference.

---

[58] These gifted men may have their impact on you via booklets, cassettes, and videos . . . but personal relationship with them on the front line of battle is really where the joy and power for effective equipping is found. Write for Foundations and Patterns for more on this.

In the end, regardless of your heart, as you speak up and break religious protocol, challenge the superficial and carnal and the shadows . . . you'll likely experience the same fate as Jesus in one way or another. "If they hated me, they will hate you also."

Don't allow men that refuse to obey Jesus put a guilt trip on you of "Division! Division!"

or, "Stay! Be patient!"

"How long?" you reply.

The unspoken answer in virtually every situation I've encountered is "Until you die of old age or your children get lulled into spiritual bankruptcy and corruption."

No way. Life is too short to be blackmailed by compromisers.

Maybe, just maybe, (lest we have the attitude of the prodigal's older brother, or those who despised the "eleventh hour workers") God will bring that camel through the eye of the needle, and a total transformation will take place where you are (if that is necessary from God's perspective). The leaven (1Cor.5:6-13) will be blown from the batch, the Life of God will pulsate in every family and gathering, and God will get all of the Glory! Do you have a heart for this?

If, instead, to your surprise, there is great resistance to the Light of exposure (John 3:19-21; 1John 1:5-9) you will be shown the door and, by God's Grace, be able to join yourself to a church that does not run from the Light. It will be worth an 80% cut in pay and a 2000 mile move, if necessary, as many on every continent can attest.

When there's work to do for our Lord, no matter what kind of group you are currently a part of, be strong and courageous and defiant of the devil who would have you be weak, dishonest, and fearful of mere men. The temptation is to keep quiet if the conversation (and "church") seems worldly, and to be frustrated or angry or depressed. If no one is honest enough to say what they are thinking, the result is a critical attitude. You know already that God can't work through that. There has to be enough honesty to shed light on the situation so that the Holy Spirit might convict and instruct those with honest hearts.

To expand on a previous point, if you do find that the nature of the time together (or the church as a whole) is somehow disappointing or even oppressive, let me encourage you again to have the Wisdom, Compassion, and Fortitude of heart to try to DRIVE it to a higher level, rather than judge or complain. It is the same no matter what type of christian group you are in. It's just that when you speak God's Word in a Filled-With-Christ-Jesus Church, you will be hugged instead of mugged.

It is far easier to point things out than it is to take responsibility to *lead* God's Lambs.   Go vertical rather than horizontal.   In other words, learn to let Jesus work through you to solve problems, rather than leaning on the natural and intellectual realms.   Cry out to Him to use a tool (maybe you!) to draw God's Lambs up to Higher Ground. From the overflow of *your* communion with God you can gently lead His Family into His Truth, Prayer to Him, or Worship of His Majesty. *Show* your brothers and sisters and neighbors an Awesome God and Tender Father, and they'll know what to do next! Asking "why?" things are too low may be right at times, but it's better by far to lift all of us Higher by taking us there.

A horizontal demand to "not be boring anymore" may backfire and add a pressure to perform.   Rather than birthing Isaac ("Laughter"), this kind of horizontal pressure to have "a better meeting" will more likely birth Ishmael (the ungodly product of man's desire and man's methods to accomplish our perception of God's desired end).   If Ishmael is force-birthed, someone will eventually take it upon himself to start a pep rally or be a self-proclaimed prophet to enliven and enlighten us.

As you find yourself in the midst of a lifeless gathering or "church," ask yourself these questions: Is the source of alienation from the Head found in unconfessed sin in the Assembly? Or might the separation from the Head be a general fatigue from consecutive late nights or even busy-ness "about the Father's Business?" (In this case, get some sleep!) Or maybe the source of the (perceived?) void of the Spirit is lack of a prayerful life or preparation on the part of those in the church?   Possibly the drought or pain is simply a "season" of dryness from God. He designed the deep valley for us to drive us to our knees, that we might ultimately move to a higher mountain than we've ever visited before.

I'm going to emphasize this point just a little more, so bear with me! We must all have discernment and deep conviction of the need to break through into reality in gatherings. Without conviction, we will not have the energy and wisdom necessary to break the curse of complacency and spectator religion that is so ingrained in us. To leave a lasting impression, I'll restate these things.

Whatever happens, please don't fake your lives together. It's not honest to pretend to have a good meeting (by hype and smiles and goo-goo faces) with everyone about to go away empty. Don't fake it. There's no merit in it and God doesn't like it anymore than we do. Please call satan on the carpet by stopping it right there and applying reality, truth and honesty to the situation. That holds true whether it's in a larger gathering or at someone's house. Take responsibility to make a difference. And, in God's timing, if it comes to this, don't be *afraid* to say (with respect and humility), "This is what I'm observing. This time together is really missing something. It seems so temporal (due to jabbering or selfishness or worldliness, or just hollowness). However, be *oh*-so-careful that you are not indicting others (or a gathering) on evidence more related to your mood, hormones, your own spiritual emptiness, or unproven discernment about spiritual matters. And, as was previously stated, better than pointing out fallacies, it is a much higher way to help others by drawing them to higher ground. Don't simply diagnose what they may already know. Overflow into the church from *your* storehouse of relationship with the Father!

In addition, if you do speak up about things that seem out of order, be careful not to carelessly offend anyone. Though it can be done, it's a rare case when you would boldly rebuke someone in public. In 1 Timothy, chapter 5, Paul taught of rebuking the elders publicly (when there were two or three witnesses) so that all the others would fear. Paul rebuked Peter publicly for being prejudiced against Gentiles. In public letters, Paul and John both called out specific men by name that were causing trouble. Jesus publicly denounced religious leaders who were not doing their jobs, in front of their "flocks."[59]   There definitely is a time for public confrontation, but be careful not to offend unnecessarily in public. Far better, when possible, to take it "to him and him alone."

Stop satan in his tracks by prayerfully and humbly opening a situation that God has called you to be involved in, and applying truth, reality and transparency. You shall know, you shall penetrate the Reality, and the Reality will set you free (Jn. 8:32). Try it. Stepping out of the show into reality and talking about what is happening at that moment in time – cracking the glossy, superficial shell – has been a vital missing ingredient that has quenched God's Spirit and ravaged the people of God.

I remember one of the first times I noticed the tragedy of being mesmerized and enslaved and robbed of our roles as a "Kingdom of Priests" by religious protocol and fear of men.   This particular situation involved a brand-new christian.   We were "attending" a meeting in a "church building" and having a "Bible Study."   Our "devotional" had three songs and a prayer and six different people giving little mini-talks; a wonderful "spiritual" event – and someone in the back row sobbing almost all of the way through it.   Here's the tragic part: nobody budged.   We were orchestrating such a grand show that we didn't have time to care for a sister who was having a hard time. She told me at that time that she was ready to walk out and not come back! She said, "I don't get it. I can't handle this anymore. I just don't get it." Now look at her! (She was sitting in the room where we were, three years later, full of Life!) There MUST be enough honesty and truthfulness to just talk!

Be the people of God; be brothers and sisters. If somebody was crying at the dinner table, I don't think we'd say, "Pass the peas, please." I don't think that we would ignore it and go on eating, do the dishes, and leave that hurting person sitting there crying at the table.   Do you?   I don't think that would happen there, so it shouldn't happen in a gathering of God's Family either. If somebody was crying in our living room, do you think we would ignore it? Can you even imagine that? Can you conceive of the possibility of having

---

[59] Matthew 23.

guests over for an evening, someone breaking into tears, and the conversation about the weather and the latest Cub's score continuing on and on? You would NEVER see that happening in a true family. And there's no reason why we should be performing a religious show and ignoring reality in true Family gatherings either. And don't wait for outward tears – even a look of disappointment or boredom or frustration should be sufficient to stop the externals in order to get to reality in a life.

(Hebrews 6:10)
   "God is not unjust; he will not forget your work and the love you have shown him as you have helped his people and continue to help them."

   Please refuse to allow ritual and false religious etiquette to hypnotize you, shanghai your walk with your God, and weaken your service of brothers and sistors!

Chapter Seventeen

Impale Detail

P RACTICAL stuff. At your gatherings, keep the trivia of every detail of your day, or even the details of your evangelistic conversations with non-Christians, to a minimum. Sometimes this might be appropriate for "equipping" reasons, but rarely. Ask for prayers if prayers are needed, but without a long story. Be considerate of others. Does anyone know what I'm talking about? When it's YOUR story, it's great. When it's someone else's story, it gets old real fast if it is not significant to the church as a whole. So be sensitive and give the bare minimum of details, unless there's reason to go beyond this. This is especially true when the numbers are very large in the gatherings of the entire church, but it remains an important principle even with "two or three gathered in His Name."

By the way, it also can be wrong and time-consuming to start asking for details that are unimportant. If prayers are requested, we don't need to ask 40 questions about the situation. Some people are very curious, while others don't need the answers to those 40 questions in order to pray for the situation. So don't get caught up in an evening of trivia talking about this and that. It isn't the Kingdom of God to be involved in trivia. Again, I'm not saying never talk about anything specific or practical (sometimes it's perfect!), but I am saying that you should be careful about needless detail controlling gatherings.

Chapter Eighteen

Jesus Christ:
Not Sigmund Freud

R EAL worship of Jesus and the penetrating applied Word of God must be the ever-dominant theme of His disciples' gathering. While, of course, there will be honesty, humility, and confession, meetings should not be "pity parties." If Christ is in it, you will find a jubilant application of the Truth of God. Even though there will be tears at times, there is Hope in Christ even in the serious and painful situations of life. Praise God!

The honest confession and heart-cry of a Saint often launches the Power of God in gatherings. The answer from the Heart of God to our struggles (when He is allowed to reign in our midst), is frequently more than anyone could "ask or imagine!"

To see mountain-top Truth explode from the Saints and shatter darkness there are at least three prerequisites:

1)   The liberty of Christ to run His own Church is such that it *allows* an occasion for brothers and sisters to really open their hearts, and,

2)   Our confident Faith in God (in spite of the circumstances).

3)   The Wonderful Counselor, by His Mercy, blessing His People.

Given the above, boy, can some awesome things occur.

As for the "confident Faith" part, you know where I'm coming from on this – a positive application of the reality of a living Jesus to whatever the problem happens to be. As we come together and "everyone has a hymn, a word of instruction, or a revelation" (the light bulb pops on: "Wow! Now I understand!"), let our expressions be a continual expression of Faith in our Father and His Only Son Jesus. Confession of sin is certainly a part of being a christian and thus an element in the church and its gatherings. Yet let it be with an expectation of the certainty of God's faithfulness to forgive, instruct, and overcome. And come with "ears to hear" what God might say through His Priesthood (the church) in response to your confession. Have an attitude of anticipation!

A letter that I received today from a companion in the Faith, a new Christian, is an example of just that kind of heart. It ended with:

"Sometimes I am almost amazed at just how messed-up I can be in this area. I am so grateful that God is an awesome God and <u>nothing</u> is too mixed-up and damaged that He can't straighten it out and heal it."

Great expression of Faith, huh? Not really. Just normal Christ-ianity!

(Hebrews 11:6)
"But without faith it is impossible to please Him, for he who comes to God must believe that He is, and that He is a rewarder of those who diligently seek Him."

(James 1:5-6)
"If any of you lacks wisdom, let him ask of God, who gives to all liberally and without reproach, and it will be given to him. But let him ask in faith, with no doubting, for he who doubts is like a wave of the sea driven and tossed by the wind."

(James 5:16)
"Confess your sins to one another, and pray for one another, that you may be healed. The effective, fervent prayer of a righteous man avails much."

"Everything must be done for the strengthening of the church" (1Cor.14:26). Follow that guideline by coming with an application of

the living Word of God, or His grace to your life – for the strengthening of the Church. Turn your life to Jesus and your deepest trials and failings will never be self-indulgent, but rather your heart will strengthen and uplift the church.

"Look how awful my trouble is and how terrible it seems . . . but through God it's a 'light and momentary' 'NBD' (no big deal) issue. Look at what God's going to do! Can you believe it? It seems impossible, but God's using it to refine me and increase my Faith as He comes through again! 'All things work together for the good for those who love Him and are called according to his purpose.' I choose to believe that. I believe God. If He created the universe, then I think He'll keep that promise in Romans 8 – so I don't have to be defeated and depressed about the circumstances. Anyone have a Word genuinely from God for me about this opponent of Faith that I've faced-off with?"

Some incredible (or as one sister said, "Credible" – since it's God!) teaching never heard from behind a pulpit has taken place at a time when a lamb opens the heartaches or failings of his life to the church. With such room to move, Jesus can do some fabulous things that 40 hours in a "study" could never *begin* to touch.[60] He can

---

[60] The "Lord of the Sabbath," on many occasions, had a different idea of what "Keep Holy the Sabbath" meant than the scholars did. Joel, chapter two, would never have been interpreted by the scholars to mean what the Holy Spirit said it meant in Acts, chapter two. Though all of the Scriptures – page after page of the Old Testament – point towards and prophesy of the Messiah, few followed Jesus on the basis of knowledge gained in a "scholarly" approach to the Bible. There was only one man that we know of that was of the "scholar class" that did not reject the very Messiah that the preachers had studied about, taught about, and waited for! Joseph of Arimathea.

God's desire is that we "abide in" – **make our home in** – His Word, not analyze it. Then, as in Acts Two, allow the Holy Spirit to say, in the context of our NEED, "This is That which was spoken of by . . . ." Jesus, alive in and amongst His People, is the key of Knowledge. He is "all wisdom and revelation." Rather than formulating our eschatalogical and other doctrinal scaffolding to reach God, let's just walk with Him!

give His servants "an instructed tongue to know the Word that sustains the weary." And real praise (rather than simply a pre-planned "praise and worship time") can then erupt from this surprising victory in a way that the most talented leader could never reproduce. Can you see it?

Many, many times Jesus has used real situations in our lives to encourage and change the whole church.

"I always seem to figure out that I've put my foot in my mouth *after* I've done the damage. Will I *ever* get to the place where I don't do that anymore?!"

The verbal answer to that simple question was captured for posterity in a booklet entitled "Levels of Maturity."

"I never feel as if I get anything out of my 'prayer' and 'Bible Study' times. Is there something wrong with me?"

The answer to that question ended up arriving in some depth a couple of days later in a gathering that was partially recorded, and called "Time Home." Because of the freedom of the gathering and the sweet sister's honesty, not only did she receive an answer, but it seemed that the entire church, some non-Christians, and other folks from out of state who were with us that day, benefitted as well.

To reinforce the point, if you will apply honesty, truth, reality, faith, life, liberty, and grace to everything that comes your way, Jesus can work through everything easily for the strengthening of the Church. Don't get caught in the trap of having simply a "sharing session" or "group therapy session" when you come together. Petition the Lord of the Harvest and turn to Him and His Church in

---

(Matthew 11:25)

At that time Jesus said, "I praise you, Father, Lord of heaven and earth, because You have hidden these things from the wise and learned, and revealed them to little children. Yes, Father, for this was your good pleasure.

"All things have been committed to Me by my Father. No one knows the Son except the Father, and no one knows the Father except the Son and those to whom the Son chooses to reveal Him."

humility and expectation even in your deepest struggles. God will hear you and shower you with Love.

Chapter Nineteen

The Perspiration of Inspiration

(Hebrews 10:24-25 Amp.)
"And let us consider and give attention, continuous care to watching over one another, studying how we may stir up (stimulate and incite and spur) one another to love and helpful deeds and noble activities, not forsaking or neglecting to assemble together as Believers . . . "

THIS is so important! **Consider:** How can I help my brothers and sisters grow? How can I spur them on? Spurs have sharp points sometimes, (HI-O Silver!) so spur one another on toward love and good deeds with creativity and imagination. Consider how you might do that! Please let me provoke you, spur you on, to unlearn the detestable religious passivity of 20th-Century spectator-christianity! Consider, give careful thought, use your imagination as to how you might spur others on. Enter into gatherings, meals, and after work stops at another brother or sister's house or apartment having *considered* how you might encourage them in Christ! Prepare yourself for life, work, grocery shopping, and gatherings, in the prayer closet – and you'll never lack for those who have been impacted by your love and service.

Many in the local expression of Christ of which I am a part have written songs and offered them as gifts to Christ in the gatherings of the Saints – even at Ben & Jerry's! (An ice cream parlor.) The poems and songs that have been written, and the paintings and drawings and other offerings to God from His family, have been a tremendous encouragement (and a welcomed, convicting challenge in some cases). Even the children have written, out of the contests that they've faced and found Christ in, some songs of victory and truth. The tremendous power and simplicity of ten-year-old Leah's song: "I will not offer to God that which costs me nothing . . ." echoes through my mind again and again some days.

Of course, don't be a show-off and don't say or do "religious" things to be noticed or to boost your ego, or bring "Cain" gifts that are only out of your own uncrucified natural abilities. But for sure *don't bury the Life that God has revealed in you!* [61] Bring on those gifts that you are offering to your God and your Family! Don't, as King David (and Leah) said, offer gifts to God that cost you nothing!

---

[61] Galatians 1:16.

Chapter Twenty

Not Slaves
To The Carnal

WATCH out for carnal dominance in meetings. You surely
have noticed that words from one whose life is hidden in
Christ are heart-rending – while the exact same words from a
self-willed, uncrucified life are like fingernails on a chalkboard. Can
you relate to that? The words aren't it. It has to do with "the spirit
and the life."

It comes in various forms:

Mr. (or Ms.) Loud,
    Mr. Opinionated,
        Mr. Talkative,
            Mr. Whine,
                Mr. Criticize,
                    Mr. Control,
Mr. Know-it-all,
    Mr. Scholar,
        Mr. Experience,
            Mr. Mega Talent,
                Mr. Insensitive,

Mr. Let's-Sing-My-Favorite-Song (I love to sing),
Mr. I-Can-Help-You-Poor-People-Out,
Mr. We've-Got-To-Be-Careful-Here,

. . . and a host of cousins and nephews.

Pray and fast. Be willing to speak about the difficulties, first
(if at all possible) "to him and him alone." Then take it to him with
two or three witnesses who can help to clarify the issue, and then
tell it to the church (Mat.18). Exercise caution here and don't *"break
the bruised reed"* or *"embitter the child."* [62] The man who Jesus

---

[62] The booklet "The Apostle Paul's Guide to Discipling Carnal Christians"
contains useful related principles.

described in the parable of the talents as the "one-talent man" was very carnal in his reaction: *"I know that you are a hard man, harvesting where you have not sown . . . so I was afraid and went out and hid your talent."* That was a carnal reaction. "I don't have to put up with this stuff. I knew you would cheat me and that you're a hard master. I just knew. Man, this stuff is no fun at all and pooey-pooey on you!" Obviously, that's a very carnal reaction.

When you take an immature and dominant brother or sister aside, the typical reaction will be:

"Who do you think you are? I don't talk anymore than anyone else! If that's the way everyone feels, I just won't talk anymore! Okay?!"

You know what I mean? (In other words, "I'll just bury my talent then!")

"I knew it; I just knew it. Forget it. I try so hard and nobody appreciates anything I do."

That's the "one-talent reaction." It's carnal and you can't win either way. What they do, they do out of carnality. When you correct them on it, they want to bury their talent. Jesus' response to talent bury-ers is *"you wicked and lazy servant. . . Throw that worthless servant outside, into the darkness, where there will be weeping and gnashing of teeth."*

Don't allow carnality, weakness and disorder to reign. It's a challenge because usually carnality, weakness and disorder want to usurp the throne. It's typically weaker brothers or weaker sisters in most churches who have the loudest voices, make the most waves, control things, and get their own way. Weakness, carnality and disorder can reign so easily, and we can't let that happen. Carnality, disorder and chaos cannot rule and reign over our meetings. It is neither loving nor compassionate to let carnality run God's Kingdom. On the other hand, do not let the one-talent (carnal) man bury his talent and thus kill himself (or herself), either.

Have fun and I wish you well.

Chapter Twenty-One

Discernment

L ET openness, honest confession of sin, prayer for health (and other petitions), and total transparency be governed by discernment – not by pride, fear or apathy. If total transparency is governed by discernment, there will be times to withhold things. For instance, the confession of sexual sins in the midst of both couples and mixed singles is usually bad discernment, because in doing that, people are easily tempted. Without desiring to do so at all, they'll think about it and the details of the confession may stick in their minds for a long time. They won't want to, but every time they see you, they may think about that confession. What you intended to be an honest and humble confession was actually creating a temptation in someone else's life. Be careful about talking about things at times and in places that would hurt other people. It's a matter of wisdom and sensitivity.

Be sure that discernment is the ruling factor, not pride, fear or apathy. Fear shouldn't keep you from confessing anything. Nor should you be too apathetic to care whether it's confessed or not. And don't keep from confessing because you are too proud to show others that you are a weak vessel at times, too. Those factors can never rule; only discernment in Christ's Spirit should rule. Understand?

If a number of large or small gatherings pass by with no confession of sin or brokenness before God (not wimpy introspection, but humility and vigorous hatred of the enemy of Jesus), I would be afraid for the life expectancy of that group. I suspect its days would be numbered – at least true Life would be near faltering. God will work with people who have messed up a hundred different ways if they'll just hate sin and confess it honestly and openly. Sin, remember, is the thing that stands between God and man. Let your humility and confession be done in Wisdom, but not rationalized into closed and hypocritical state.

When God is on the Throne and we come easily, with freedom and discernment, into the Light . . . He Himself will join us. And you can't beat that!

Chapter Twenty-Two

Where Do Women Fit In?

C ERTAINLY the question of a "woman's role" will come up, and
justifiably so. There is very good reason for the woman's role
to be discussed in regard to meetings. We know that Paul saw fit to
write about it a number of times, and we too should recognize it as
a very important Biblical issue; let's not pretend it doesn't matter.

Paranoia, arrogance, ignorance of the Scriptures, and the
traditions of men are four foes in this battle to understand the
women's role, each leading to a different way of missing God.

Paranoia is that opponent of Truth and of a Celebration of
God's Spirit where men run from anything that looks like it might
be trouble. "Better safe than sorry" is an ungodly motto of cowards
and faithless men and women. In this mode we will stifle anything
and everything that God may wish to do in our generation. Had the
father of our Faith, Abraham, had this attitude towards God and the
things of God, Abraham would never have taken Isaac to that
mountain to be sacrificed. ("That's murder - God judged Cain
severely for such an act of wickedness.") David would surely not
have danced as he celebrated before the Ark. ("Moses never did
that. It's unauthorized.") John would have been labeled an
unbiblical fool for claiming that men should be baptized by him,
since there was no Scripture in existence in his day to support such
an idea. God's viewpoint was quite different. Any who rejected
John's baptism "rejected God's purpose for their lives" (according to
God Himself), even though John baptized without any written
"authorization" and no "signs and wonders" to prove himself. Am I
saying "anything goes?" No way. I am saying, however, that our
mortal interpretation of the Scriptures is so woefully shallow that we
had better not create a rigid system of "the way things must be to
please God" and allow our paranoia to cheat us out of God's
Blessings. And in this case, rob women of their responsibilities as
Priestesses in the Kingdom.

Arrogance is enemy number two. Some in this camp do not actually care what the Bible says about this matter because, after all, any limitation of women's roles is probably just a cultural thing, anyway. "I have my rights, you know." "Paul was a chauvinist." Please do not exalt yourself above God and His Word in this way. "The Word was with God; the Word was God." Careless arrogance is a lethal position to take.

And **Ignorance** of the Scriptures leads to chaos. We make our own way and our own rules when we do not "make our home in His Word" and, instead, do whatever seems right in our own eyes. That's clearly not God's Will, either.

Traditions of Men, enemy number four, still, as Jesus said, make "null and void" the Word of God. It doesn't matter one lick what you're "comfortable" with, or the way pappy used to do it. Shocking? Seek God's Face, not your own comfort zone. No one who followed after Jesus, in the days He visited this planet in the flesh, bypassed being shocked at His "unorthodox" interpretations and practices. Jesus hasn't changed. Prepare to be shocked . . . and follow anyway.

These four foes must all be crushed in order to know God's Way for our lives and His church. In a formal "service," complete with a pre-programmed liturgy of songs, prayers and actors, "what role should women take" is an even tougher question. When you have a pre-set format, a printed program that's handed out at the door, and people assigned to certain roles, many situations are far more complicated than they need to be. "Who will play thus and such a role? Do I dare allow a woman to say a prayer?" Since the institutional structure was never God's intention in the first place, of course it is hard to know what God's Will for the role of women is in that format! When you have a liturgy and a religious machine instead of the Family of God, it creates unnecessary tensions. In the context of life in Christ, it's not a difficult question to resolve.[63] When the people of God are functioning in Life, as a family, without pomp and circumstance and a program, the question can be approached from a simple family standpoint. When you have a

---

[63] If this subject is one that is important to you, you might find the two-tape cassette series Silent Women in the Church helpful.

program, a system and a machine, big-time decisions have to be made. When you're living life together as Family, God works through that to answer a lot of questions.

Wherever you happen to be, I suggest that you yield to the leadership of that assembly on this point of a woman's role. And yield to it enthusiastically, whatever they decide. If you choose to be a part of that local body, under the local expression of the government of Jesus (Isa.9:7; Heb.13:7, 17; Heb.12:15), be an asset to the unity and corporate life of Jesus there, not a thorn.

Simply for information's sake, the way we have learned to relate to each other in the church here is that the women, so as not to "dishonor her head," "the man," (1Cor.11:5, 3, 8-9; 1Tim.2:11-15) never barges in during a gathering and takes control of a point being made or during times we are turning vertically towards God. She is never to have an outspoken, authoritative presence in a meeting, as if "over" (rather than "submissive to") the men present.[64] There *is* to be a difference, Biblically, between men's and women's roles in the Church – no question about it. A woman should ask, "May we pray?" rather than "Let us pray." "May we sing 'Majesty'?" rather than simply starting the song as many of the brothers do. With the right heart, even "May I share this scathing rebuke that God has put on my heart about . . .?" is not "usurping" if it is the Will of God and acceptable to the men to say what she's seen. (In fact, it would be "unsubmissive" to *not* share what is on her heart if the men ask her to.) It's okay if it's done in humility, with graciousness, beauty and honor. If a woman is, out of frustration or pride, trying to fill the men's role, God can not use her to do what *she* is called to do. When everyone is filling the part that God designed for him or her (such a rarity!) it is astonishing how things fit together. God is honored, and everyone is fulfilled.

We should note, as we ponder this challenge, that the very nature of the second (and last) Covenant includes a prominent place for women. At least part of their role is described by the Holy Spirit as:

---

[64] 1Timothy 2:11-12.

(Acts 2:15-21)
   *"Your sons and your daughters will tell forth the divine counsels
. . . even on my servants, both men and women, I will pour out my
Spirit in those days and they will tell forth the divine counsels."*

   1 Corinthians 11:5 speaks of women praying and prophesying.
It is highly likely that men were present, or the entire reason for
writing the warning (the danger of "dishonoring" the woman's head,
the man) would have been of little relevance. Twenty-five years after
Pentecost the evangelist Philip had four daughters who prophesied
(Acts 21:8-9).

   These Scriptures, at least, do seem to venture beyond much
of christendom's normal conception of "women in the church."

   Another entire segment of christendom has very little respect
for the Scriptures, and just collapses into "conforming to the patterns
of the world." Anything that the world allows or demands eventually
becomes acceptable for these false churches. An expanding role for
women in society and business seems to "re-write" the Scriptures in
groups such as this.

   I believe you'll find, as you consider God's Word on the
subject, that gatherings like those on Solomon's Porch (Jerusalem,
mega-thousands present, Acts 2 - 5) and the "whole church"
gatherings (Corinth, numbers unknown, 1 Cor.14:23), the "daily in
public" part of "daily in public and from house to house" will work
out to be a little different than the "house to house" gatherings as far
as the women's part goes. While just as free (1 Cor.14:26 is a "whole
church" passage), the possibilities of "dishonoring the head" (1 Cor.11)
are much higher – and different cautions to the women are in order
in this larger environment. Think about it; pray about it.

   In spite of all of the pressures of the man-made rules or
liberties, women must be women who tell forth the divine counsels
of God. That's the nature of the New Testament church, prophesied
by Joel and repeated by Peter in Acts 2. The nature of the New
Testament church includes both sons and daughters – both men and
women, telling forth the divine counsels of God. God's Will is that
women, and men too, function out of humility, but *do function.*
Don't stop. Don't bury your talent. Find the way and the place that
seems good to the Holy Spirit and to you and the Family of God

(Acts 15:28; Heb.13:7, 17), and is obviously consistent with the Scriptures.[65]

---

[65] Again, let me encourage you to write and ask for <u>Silent Women in the Church</u> if this seems difficult for you. You will find considerably more depth and discussions of 1Timothy, chapter 2, and 1 Corinthians, chapter 14 on these tapes.

Chapter Twenty-Three

"From HIM" . . .
Minute By Minute

T HE meetings will be stale if everything is not "from Him and through Him and to Him." You may do something new and exciting, or new and improved, and it will be okay for a little while – maybe a month, two months, three months. But after the novelty wears off it will be stale and lifeless if times together are not "from Him and through Him and to Him." We need Him! We must be continually responsive to Him, our Risen Brother, the Head of the Church who is present in the room where we're gathering "in His Name!" Having a meeting FOR Him rather than WITH Him will quickly degenerate and rot. Worship and adore HIM – Vertically! Ask Him questions! You can easily recognize in five minutes whether a meeting is merely FOR Jesus, in His honor, (which may sound good, but alone is empty and wrong), or whether it is WITH Jesus ("from Him and through Him and to Him") as the Head, living and reigning over His church and His meeting.

How?

Here is a question that I hope you will allow to sink deeply into your heart and mind. Don't let this one slip by. See if you can answer it in your mind's eye. *"If Jesus didn't come to the meeting (Mat.18:20), would anything be different? Would we notice?"* Be honest. Would we know it if Jesus didn't come to a meeting? Or would it not matter because He hadn't been Head of the church and Head of the meeting all along anyway? "For as many as are led by the Spirit of God, they are sons of God."

Just food for thought.

"Even though we speak like this, dear friends, we are confident of better things in your case."

When Jesus *is* on the Throne, and His Priests are blowing away the enemy with Spiritual Weapons,[66] any need can be met, any question answered – all things spiritual, physical, or emotional can be touched in an incredibly unique and powerful way by the Master! Don't miss it!

---

[66] (2Cor.10:4-5) "For though we live in the world, we do not wage war as the world does. The weapons that we fight with are not the weapons of this world. On the contrary, they have supernatural power to the tearing down of strongholds."

Chapter Twenty-Four

Eyes For The Field!

I F our gatherings are to be full of Life and popping with the revelation of the Son through the gifts we bring, we must be practically involving ourselves in "bringing many sons to Glory." God will see to it that things grow stale without this. Thank Him for it!

Remember what Jesus said about His Presence in gatherings? "When you gather yourselves together in My Name, I will come into your midst." There is an interesting and helpful Truth that you should know about gathering (or praying) "in His Name." If we're not "called according to His purposes," living for what He lived for ("seeking and saving that which is lost," living to "preach good news to the poor, to proclaim freedom for the prisoners . . . "), then we're not meeting "in His Name." Remember that gathering "in His Name" is a prerequisite for His Presence (1Cor.5:4; Mat.16:18).

Meeting "in His Name" does not mean putting a sign over the door. It means that whatever Jesus represents, we also represent. We are investing our lives in the character of Christ. We are actively and continually seeking His purposes and giving Him honor with each of our lives. When you pray a prayer, and finish with "In Jesus' name, Amen," it is not a fancy way to say, "Roger, over and out." What you are really saying is (if your heart and your understanding are in order): "To You be the glory, honor and power forever and ever. This is for You; not my will but Yours be done. I'm wearing Your Name. It is Your Will that I represent, not my own motives, and so I ask with the authority of the Name of Christ. For His sake, not mine. So be it!"

And so it must be when we gather, representing what He represents, or He is not "in our midst." If He is not truly in our midst, the "Power of the Lord Jesus present" (1Cor.5:4, 4:20) must be artificially simulated by the props and programs, the shrewdly crafted "worship experience" and the powerful "sermon."

If I sent you to the bank with a check that I had signed, you could take money out of the bank, right? You're my representative; there is an ambassadorship going on. You are "authorized," endued with "authority" in my name. And when you pray in His Name, you are investing yourself in His Character and His Purpose.

You can pray selfishly and never get an answer.

"You do not have, because you do not ask God. When you ask, you do not receive, because you ask with wrong motives, that you may spend what you get on your pleasures."

"Wait a minute," you say. "I thought I could ask anything I wanted in His Name and it would be received!" The difference is that when you ask according to His Will, He hears you (1 John 5) – and that's when you are truly praying in His Name. You are coming as an authentic representative of HIS Kingdom. That's what it means to pray or to meet together "in His Name."

If we are gathered in His Name, we are gathered for His Purpose. What is His Purpose? Among His prime purposes was His devotion to "seek and save that which is lost." His heart was to "bring many sons to Glory." His purpose was to preach good news to the poor and recovery of sight to the blind, and declare the year of the Lord's favor. We're not meeting in His Name if our purpose for existing isn't the same as His – to bring many sons to Glory (not even just to salvation, but to a full expression of His Life – to "Glory").

If loving Him and what He loves is not our reason for living, our meetings will surely grow to be stale and empty (unless pumped up with flesh, drama, and programs). You may notice that if you're not reaching out to people and living the Christ-life outside of meetings, they get more and more boring, quickly. And internal strife begins to be manifested. Inwardness always brings about a corrupted mutation eventually. These heartbreaking developments are a gift from God – flags along the road to let us know of our deviation from His Course. We are only meeting in His Name as far as we are serving His Purposes. And He only promises to be in our midst when we are meeting in His Name for His current Intents.[67]

---

[67] Somehow, some have thought that if we have the right components of worship, "worship" in the "scriptural" way, God will automatically be there. Don't be fooled! Our worship can be 100% "scriptural" and even "exciting" and Jesus not be there. That is, if we're not meeting in HIS Name and called according to HIS

Does that make sense? And when He's not with us, wherever we are is a lousy place to be. You know what I mean.

When He *is* in our midst, there will always be surprises, special joys. Maybe a brother or sister who is generally relatively quiet will burst forth with something from Heaven (a song they've written, a poem, an unexpected Word to the weary, a Faith-filled confession and expression of praise). Often Light from God's realm will expose and reveal in spectacular ways that set long-bound prisoners free! "Times of refreshing come from repentance." When He is in our midst, we may see conversions in a mighty way. Or he lifted with great laughter and jubilation. We may be visited by "an angel unawares." There may be a "sending out" of the entire church (the adults) into the bars on a Friday night. Or, with the young ones, to the alleys and sewer grates where the street people make their homes. God has been gracious to allow His Saints in many cities and countries to see these things, and many more . . . . What else is out there for His Church, wherever she has chosen His Best?! I really do want to find out. God help us and sustain us.

Christ "circulates amongst the Lampstands" (Rev. 2:1-5; Mat. 18:20).[68] In Ephesus they were doing some wonderfully "scriptural" things. They were benevolent, evangelistic and energetic in all of their ways. Great stuff was going on. However, they lost their first love and their Lampstand was going to be taken away. Christ only circulates amongst the Lampstands. Although the meeting may have been scriptural, they were going to lose their right to be the church of Jesus Christ because their first love wasn't Jesus Himself. They were going to lose their right to have Christ circulate in their midst . . . and that could happen with a 100% "scriptural" meeting. Without Jesus truly being here, this church will become a yucky "religious" place to be. And I, for one, wouldn't want to be a part of anything that He is not a part of.

---

purposes.

[68] The booklet <u>Apostolic Foundations and Apostolic Patterns</u> goes into a significant amount of detail about this matter, and what a "church," a "Lampstand," truly is, from God's perspective.

Our "Bread," our Manna, our nourishment from God is to "do the Will of the One Who has sent us, and to FINISH His Work."[69] The Power of God is found only by gathering "in His Name" – existing for the sole purpose of *doing* His Will! Plug in!

---

[69] John 4:32-35; Mat.4:4; Philemon 6; Acts 1:8.

Strength
for the Battle

His truths God's entrusted
to those He has named.
They're clearly recorded,
But rarely proclaimed.

Truths that inspire us,
Make us fall on our knees;
Truths that are glorious,
Truths such as these –

The Creator majestic,
His glorious Son,
The Spirit who counsels,
Three persons in One.

The Father who loves us
Extends us His hands,
And to save us from harm
Gives us loving commands.

The Spirit, Convictor,
Awakening One,
Who shows us our sins
And points toward the Son.

Christ Jesus, the King,
the Ender of Strife,
Redeemer of sin,
And Giver of Life,

To those who will follow,
Repent of their sin,
Be washed with pure water,
Forsake everything,

He gives them a new life;
He births them again,
Into a kingdom
Unknown by mere men.

It's a kingdom of love
Where we feed on His bread.
The redeemed form a body
Of which He's the head.

In the kingdom, He comforts,
In the kingdom, He rules;
He shapes and transforms us,
Makes us His tools.

These truths are indeed glorious,
A lamp for our feet.
They inspire and strengthen
Until we're complete.

These truths God's entrusted
To those He has named.
They're clearly recorded,
But rarely proclaimed.

Rarely proclaimed on the
job or at home,
In the streets or the market
Or to those trapped alone.

For speaking is risking
With subjects as these.
Confrontation invited
Unsteadies our knees.

The mind is convinced
To speak these truths bold,
But as the moment approaches
The heart will grow cold.

Self will assert itself,
Brilliantly plead
To silence the tongue
And postpone the deed.

For where the realms of ideas
And actions meet
There is a battleground
Fervent with heat.

Too many speak boldly
When no foes are in sight,
And think themselves soldiers
Of the Forces of Light.

But bravado in barracks
Will not meet the need.
What's needed is courage
In word and in deed.

Overcomers are needed,
Overcomes this day,
Whose love for their Lord
Makes them join in the fray.

Willing to venture,
Willing to dare,
To speak for the One
They've entrusted their care.

God's overcomer-
is he fearless and sure?
Free from infirmities,
Not needing a cure?

Oh, no, he is different,
Far different indeed!
He's sure of his weakness,
Convinced of his need.

"Christ Jesus, Lord Jesus,
Please help me!" he cries,
And with unsteady knees
And stomach's butterflies,

He opens his mouth,
God's truths to express,
And words are soon given
To rightly address

The one now before him,
A captive to sin.
He tells him of Jesus
and bids him come in.

Into the kingdom
Of light and of love,
The gift of the Father
in heaven above.

He's often rejected,
Insulted and jeered.
Though outwardly wounded,
He's inwardly cheered.

Cheered by the strength
Christ freely gave,
And the knowledge that his God
Is mighty to save.

Great power will God
Entrust to his care.
Faithful he is,
Much fruit he will bear.

Since the time of our Lord
The battle's the same.
Satan conspires
To silence His Name.

Would you the life of
An Overcomer live?
Your life you must lose
And your heart you must give.

To Him, who despite all
Was Faithful and True,
And overcame death
And Satan for you.

To obey Him in danger
When fears abound,
You must obey Him in safety
When no one's around.

For God's overcomer
Is a worshipper first.
His failures he knows,
But he's filled with a thirst

For God's kingdoms in heaven
and earth to be one.
He gives God no rest
Until it is done.

Be faithful, my brothers.
Deliver His Word.
Faithful, though fearful,
Hold fast to your Lord.

All in the great cloud
Had moments of fear,
But serve Him they did.
For their Savior was near.

On the foolishness of words
Does man's destiny depend.
Let the Spirit through your words
A broken heart mend.

Cry out for His love;
Cry out for His zeal.
Be one through whom God
Can make His appeal.

Kevin

Chapter Twenty-Five

A "Neither Here, Nor There" Kingdom

I T would be best to elaborate in a practical way, with your permission, a little more on the following point. The real McCoy, a true expression of God's reign and "Dwelling Place" amongst His People (Eph 2:22) will not wait for the gavel to pound for the beginning of a meeting. As the People of God, we'll be singing or praying together in smaller groups continually as a life, without any cues or "meetings" to set us up for that. "As we rise up, as we sit down, as we walk along the way." In living rooms, in restaurants together - or even in jail together (Acts 16:25-26)! We will be singing the praises of God inside and outside of "meetings" . . . because it's our life.

I don't mean this in a sappy, theoretical way. I'm serious! There's really no "opening song" (or "song service") or "closing prayer" in the Churches that are really walking with a living Head, rather than in uplifting historical observances and good intentions. Life is a song to Him when we "live and move and have our being in Him" - continually offering our bodies as "living sacrifices." If we are really on target, we'll sing to Jesus when we're alone with Him, and we'll sing with our brothers and sisters at Burger King, and virtually anywhere. We may be singing before 8:30 P.M. or 9:00 A.M. or whenever the gathering happens. "Church" is meant to be our life, not a number of independent lives and gatherings that are "vain repetition" - a protestant version of the rosary. "It was not so from the beginning."

We will, if immersed in Jesus and His Purposes, be praying together continually, all the days of the week. There will be no thought of the "official" meeting as the limit or focal point of our adoration, and work for, the Lord. We could *easily* find ourselves together all night.[70] Why? Because that's Who Jesus was and is, and we are filled with Him if we are truly Christians.[71]

Jesus said, "My Father's House shall be known as a house of prayer." That's a characteristic of God's Kingdom. It's a house of prayer. It does not consist of even frequent or all night "prayer meetings" – it is a "house of prayer." If we are His, we'll be living it out, not in "meetings" only, but "daily in public and from house to house," and "Holy-Spiriting[72] one another daily so that none are hardened by sin's deceitfulness."

True "Church" is a visible life, "a city set on a hill that cannot be hidden" where "all men" know we are His disciples by the love that they see we have for one another.[73] Your love, your agape for each other, will blow the world's cork. They won't understand how you could keep no record of wrongs, always hope, and always trust. If the world can't see it happening (though they can harden themselves if they desire), then it is not Jesus. If the meetings are truly worth anything at all in God's sight, then the "Church" must emanate the visible Life of Christ Jesus on the streets of life, together.

God's Church, the blossom of His Life continued on earth, was never meant to be a theory that we study about in a classroom. In Acts 2:41-47 and 4:31-35, they held all things in common (out of a life surrendered to Jesus, not church ordinance). They shared their very lives together, and "they enjoyed the favor of all the people." People could *see* the Kingdom of God happening.

"Church," from God's vantage point, must be a visible thing to the world; it's not simply attending "meetings." His true church goes far beyond meetings and programs! His Kingdom is "not of this

---

[70] Acts 12:5-6, 12; Acts 20:7-12; Mat.21:13.

[71] Col.1:26-27; Rom.8:9-11; John 14:9-24; Eph.5:18.

[72] Hebrews 3:12-14. The word used in verse 13 is the verb form of the Name Jesus used to describe the Holy Spirit and His Work – "Paraclete" (Greek), "Comforter," "Called-Along-Side One."

[73] Matthew 5:14-16; Matthew 16:18; John 13:34-35; 1Peter 2:9-12.

world," "not in Jerusalem, or on this mountain," not from 9 A.M. to 11 A.M. on the corner of thus and such a street. That is simply not His Kingdom if it can be defined by times and places, and a "serve-us" schedule on a calendar. No such church can be found in the pages of the Bible! Moses allowed it because of the hardness of our hearts, but "not so with you." "It was not so in the beginning." *"In Him we live and move and have our being!"*

Chapter Twenty-Six

Leadership

(2Samuel 23:3-4)

"The God of Israel said, the Rock of Israel spoke to me: 'He who rules over men must be just, ruling in the fear of God. And he shall be like the light of the morning when the sun rises, a morning without clouds, Like the tender grass springing out of the earth, by clear shining after rain.'"

(Judges 2:18-19)

"And when the Lord raised up judges for them, the Lord was with the judge and delivered them out of the hand of their enemies all the days of the judge; for the Lord was moved to pity by their groaning because of those who oppressed them and harassed them. And it came to pass, when the judge was dead, that they reverted and behaved more corruptly than their fathers, by following other gods, to serve them and bow down to them. They did not cease from their own doings nor from their stubborn way."

(Exodus 30:31-33)

"Say to the Israelites, 'This is to be my sacred anointing oil for the generations to come. Do not pour it on men's bodies and do not make any oil with the same formula. It is sacred, and you are to consider it sacred. Whoever makes any [counterfeit anointing oil] like it or whoever puts any of it on an outsider, shall be cut off from his people.'"

(Ezekiel 44:7-9)

"In addition to all your other detestable practices, you brought foreigners uncircumcised in heart and flesh into my sanctuary, desecrating my temple while you offered me food, fat and blood, and you broke my covenant. Instead of carrying out your duty in regard to my holy things, you put others in charge of my sanctuary. This is what the Sovereign Lord says: No foreigner uncircumcised in heart and flesh is to enter my sanctuary, not even the foreigners who live among the Israelites."

(1Samuel 10:6-7)

"The Spirit of the Lord will come upon you in power, and you will prophesy with them; and you will be changed into a different person. Once these signs are fulfilled, do whatever your hand finds to do, for God is with you."

(1Kings 13:33-34)

"Even after this, Jeroboam did not change his evil ways, but once more appointed priests for the high places from all sorts of people. Anyone who wanted to become a priest he consecrated for the high places. This was the sin of the house of Jeroboam that led to its downfall and to its destruction from the face of the earth."

(1Chronicles 15:12-13)

He said to them, "You are the heads of the Levitical families; you and your fellow Levites are to consecrate yourselves and bring up the ark of the Lord, the God of Israel, to the place I have prepared for it. It was because you, the Levites, did not bring it up the first time that the Lord our God broke out in anger against us. We did not inquire of him about how to do it in the prescribed way."

(Numbers 11:17)

"I will come down and speak with you there, and I will take of the Spirit that is on you and put the Spirit on them. They will help you carry the burden of the people so that you will not have to carry it alone."

(Psalms 78:72)

"And David shepherded them with integrity of heart; with skillful hands he led them."

(Genesis 41:38)

Then Pharaoh said to his servants, "Can we find such a one as this, a man in whom is the Spirit of God?"

(Romans 10:15)

And how shall they proclaim unless they are sent? As it is written: "How beautiful are the feet of those who preach the gospel of peace, who bring glad tidings of good things!"

(Galatians 1:15-16)
"But it pleased God, who separated me from my mother's womb and called me through His grace, to reveal His Son in me, that I might proclaim Him among the nations."

(1Thessalonians 2:4)
"But we have been approved by God to be entrusted with the good news, even so we speak, not as pleasing men, but God who tests our hearts."

(Hebrews 5:4-5)
"No one takes this honor upon himself; he must be called by God, just as Aaron was. So Christ also did not exalt Himself to be made a High Priest."

(Luke 9:62)
But Jesus said to him, "No one, having put his hand to the plow, and looking back, is fit for the kingdom of God."

(Luke 6:39-40)
He also told them this parable: "Can a blind man lead a blind man? Will they not both fall into a pit? A student is not above his teacher, but everyone who is fully trained will be like his teacher."

(Acts 6:2-7)
"Then the twelve summoned the multitude of the disciples and said, 'It is not desirable that we should leave the word of God and serve tables. Therefore, brethren, seek out from among you seven men of good reputation, full of the Holy Spirit and wisdom, whom we may appoint over this business; but we will give ourselves continually to prayer and to the ministry of the word.' And the saying pleased the whole multitude."

"And they chose Stephen, a man full of faith and the Holy Spirit, and Philip, Prochorus, Nicanor, Timon, Parmenas, and Nicolas, a proselyte from Antioch, whom they set before the apostles; and when they had prayed, they laid hands on them. And the word of God spread, and the number of the disciples multiplied greatly in Jerusalem, and a great many of the priests were converted to the faith."

T HE point in bringing all of these particular Scriptures, Words from Heaven, to your attention? Simply to make this statement extremely clear: No one is to be put "in charge" of anything in the kingdom of God who isn't visibly "full of the Holy Spirit and wisdom." *Men, who clearly have what Stephen had, are the minimum requirement for being "over" any matter, according to the Scriptures.* And Stephen was, visibly, *"a man full of God's grace and power."* In his testimony against the religious powers of his day, Stephen spoke such that *"they could not stand up against his wisdom or the Spirit by which he spoke."* A normal "full of the Holy Spirit" man. A "man of war" against the darkness around him.

The kind of man that God whisks up into His full Glory the way He did Enoch,[74] are men with Enoch's heart:

> *"Enoch, the seventh from Adam, prophesied about these men:* '*See! The Lord is coming with thousands upon thousands of His Holy ones to judge everyone, and to convict all the ungodly of all the ungodly acts they have done in the ungodly way, and of all the harsh words ungodly sinners have spoken against Him.'"*

There must be that fervor and "consuming zeal for the Father's House," and that ability to "See!" if we are to be of any use to God! Is that you? Could you have said, without knowing that this Scripture was in the Bible, what Enoch said? If you have what he had you could (and likely would)!

Men who are truly drunk on the Holy Spirit are easily *recognizable*, according to Acts 6. They emanate the power and refreshment of the Holy Spirit, and the Character of Jesus Christ. *"Rivers of Alive Water gush from their inner being."* The River of Life that flows from them will bring healing to those around them.

> *"And it shall be that every living thing that moves, wherever the rivers go, will live. There will be a very great multitude of fish, because these waters go there; for they will be healed, and everything will live wherever the river goes. Their fish will be . . . exceedingly many. Along the river, on this side and that, will grow all kinds of trees*

---

[74] Genesis 5:24; Heb.11:5-6; Jude 14-16.

*used for food; their leaves will not wither, and their fruit
will not fail. They will bear fruit every month, because
their water flows from the sanctuary. Their fruit will be
for food, and their leaves for medicine."*

Do you know anyone like that? Do you know men and women
who make satan tremble? Do you have a relationship with men and
women who know Jesus such that when they enter a room, with
them comes a "darkness-shattering Light?" Only such men are to be
over any matter in the Kingdom of God. *Bible knowledge is
meaningless apart from this.* Satan mocks those that are not truly
walking in *"the Power of an Indestructible Life," "full of the Holy Ghost
and Wisdom"* but presume to be leaders because they have some kind
of "training."

*And the evil spirit answered and said, "Jesus I know, and
Paul I know; but who are you?"* [75]

Good intentions, sincerity, a degree in Bible (or "spiritual"
Psychology – today's "medicine man"), worldly leadership qualities,
money . . . none of these will be any more than a joke to satan. **The
only authority in God's Kingdom is in the Anointing – His current
confirmation.** Only a man visibly "full of the Holy Ghost and
Wisdom" can be "over" any matter in the Kingdom of God. Unless,
of course, we start our own kingdom and call it by Jesus' Name.
Then, I suppose, we can do anything that we want.

*"The Spirit of the Lord God is upon Me, because the Lord
has anointed Me to preach good tidings to the poor; He
has sent Me to heal the brokenhearted, to proclaim liberty
to the captives, and the opening of the prison to those
who are bound; to proclaim the acceptable year of the
Lord, and the day of vengeance of our God; to comfort all
who mourn, to console those who mourn in Zion, to give
them beauty for ashes, the oil of joy for mourning, the
garment of praise for the spirit of heaviness; that they may
be called trees of righteousness, the planting of the Lord,
that He may be glorified. And they shall rebuild the old
ruins, they shall raise up the former desolations, and they*

---

[75] Acts 19:13-20.

shall repair the ruined cities, the desolations of many
generations. . . . But you shall be named the Priests of
the Lord, men shall call you the Servants of our God.
Instead of your shame you shall have double honor, and
instead of confusion they shall rejoice in their portion.
Therefore in their land they shall possess double;
everlasting joy shall be theirs."

A man "full of the Holy Spirit and Wisdom" is a remarkable
man. And far too rare in our day. Nevertheless, only such as he is
allowed to be "over" any matter, even as seemingly insignificant as
"waiting on tables" at a meal for widows (the Acts 6 example).

Today, "pulpits" are often filled with men not the slightest bit
"full of the Holy Spirit." (As you may have ascertained, to have a
man stand in front of a crowd of Christians and deliver a Sunday
morning speech to them is not God's idea.) The "men's business
meetings" and elders' and deacons' boards of much of today's
"church" usually have none of the marks of anything more than a
social club with religious jargon and worldly means. Even "good and
honest men" are insufficient for the task of "destroying the works of
the devil." Today's religion which assigns men to lead singing or
worship, women to teach "Bible classes," men to take charge of the
"building and grounds" (and every other "over this matter" area that
you can think of) should at least take note of the fact that any
responsibility in God's Kingdom requires true authority in the
spiritual realm in order to be successful. Why?

(Ephesians 6:12)
    "For we do not wrestle against flesh and blood, but against
principalities, against powers, against the rulers of the darkness of this
age, against spiritual hosts of wickedness in the heavenly places."

In David's day, those who were "over" the matter of music had
to be of "prophet status" – a "seer" (1Chron. 25:1, 2, 3, 5-7, etc.).
Likewise, today, a man in responsibility must have a prophetic heart;
a teachable, crucified, consecrated heart on fire for Jesus Christ. He
must have an "open heaven" and live in holiness. ("Without holiness
no one can see the Lord.") Unless one is born of water and the
Spirit, Jesus declared that he or she cannot see the Kingdom. That's
for all of us. He went on to tell us how everyone that is Born of the

Spirit would Live. He said that the Wind blows wherever it pleases. You hear its sound, but you cannot tell where it comes from or where it is going. You see the force; you see the Power behind it. And so it is with EVERYONE BORN OF THE SPIRIT (John 3:5-8). That's the kind of person who can see the Throne of God and will "speak only what he hears the Father speaking." He's one who's seated in the Most Holy Place and is eating hidden manna (Mat.4:4; Jn.4:32; Heb.9:2-5). That person is the only person who is allowed to be in charge of anything in the Kingdom of God.[76]

I've found that a good number of people, because of fear and pride, balk at these Truths. Some, whose salaries would be jeopardized if anyone acted on these Truths, will be fighting mad. Nevertheless, to be qualified to wait on tables, you have to be full of the Holy Spirit and full of Wisdom (Acts 6:3). In order to be in charge of anything in the Kingdom of God, you had better be brimming with the heart and fruit and Words of Christ, and have a Life currently before the Father in the Holy of Holies.

You know man. Man, in his state of "futile thinking" (as Paul once said), thinks that the best way to function in the "church" is to get as many people involved as possible in the "work of the Church." Then they'll be motivated. That's wrong. Dead wrong. It will be the downfall of any church to "try to get people involved," and overlook the fact that they are not brimming with the Holy Spirit and Wisdom. To "get a person involved" in positions that are visible and responsible, who is not living a full devotion to Christ and displaying the eternal fruit of that kind of life, is serious trouble. I personally don't want to answer to God for starting a "Hypocrites in Training" Program. Don't do it! No matter how tempting. Hold your ground, or you (as well as they themselves) will suffer the consequences later on.

A man capable of writing psalms with the depth of Asaph's (Ps.73-83) had the kind of heart that David entrusted with "overseeing" an area. How much more would a "leader" in a New

---

[76] More encouragement about the call of Leadership from the Word of God is available in the cassette tapes entitled: Leadership: As the Lion of Judah; Leadership: As the Murdered Lamb; Leadership: When Sent, Satan Falls; and Apostolic Foundations and Apostolic Patterns.

Covenant church have the heart and depth to speak and write psalms like Asaph did?! Heman was the King's Seer; Jeduthun was the King's Seer; Asaph was the King's Seer.[77] Notice any pattern? Those three men were the ones who were entrusted to be "over the matter" that had come up.

The same goes, of course, for "waiting on tables" – even "menial" matters in the Church. You must be the King's "Seer," one who really knows God and can "see the invisible"[78] to wait on tables, according to Acts 6:3. Doesn't it seem as if being head busboy is a job that anyone can do? Perhaps find someone with restaurant experience who can get an ego boost by "getting involved?" No big deal? Frankly, it really doesn't seem like it should be a big deal, to the natural mind. Yet, according to the Holy Spirit, to be qualified for such a "trivial" thing as this, one must be overflowing with the Heart of God. And be so to the extent that everybody knows it; they can see it; it's obvious and observable. If you can be told to "select from yourselves seven men full of the Holy Spirit and full of wisdom," it must be a discernable, obvious quality that people can see.

Now, as then, if these men and women who you are considering for some kind of responsibility are not shattering the Darkness in an observable way, you must not select them to be "over" any matter whatsoever. They mustn't presume to be, nor be asked to be, "teachers" or even head busboys.

Just for illustration's sake, imagine again the scenario in Acts, chapter six where seven men were chosen to "wait on tables." Imagine that the thousands came back to their leaders with seven men, as requested. They introduced the seven they had selected to John, Thomas, Peter, and the others with these words:

> "These are not exactly bursting with Holy Spirit power per se, but they are honest and sincere men; they would do anything for you. And they do know their Bibles real good."

---

[77] 1Chronicles 25.

[78] Hebrews 11:25-28.

There could be no other response from the men of God than:

"No way! I love these brothers, too, but GOD said 'Bursting with power from on High – full of the Holy Spirit and Wisdom!' None of us are free to water down the Word from the Lord, our King, even with good intentions!"

One clear reason why men in leadership must walk in God's Presence and Fullness: a man can't take someone to a place he has never been himself. If you want to bring someone into the Throne Room of God, you've got to first be there yourself (Psalm 43:3-4; John 1:4). To ask someone to bring you into the Throne Room of God in any area of "ministry" who isn't living there is foolishness. His level of talent or sincerity or scholarship (or even "evangelistic success") is not the issue in a Kingdom that "is not of this world."

The blind man who cannot see God will cause everyone who follows him to fall into the ditch. Jesus Himself said that. If you're blind to the Unseen World in certain areas, you may be just as saved as the next guy, but back off from leadership roles. Of course continue to offer your life and what God has done in you – in humility. But do not yield to the awesome temptation to accept an invitation to be "over" some matter before your time. And take personal responsibility to not allow someone to be over anything even as simple as "waiting on tables" without being "full of the Holy Spirit and Wisdom." Talent or willingness or training or biblical knowledge are not enough! The standard is this: VISIBLY drunk with the Holy Spirit and pressing hard towards the full measure of the stature and fruitfulness of Christ (Eph. 5:17-18, 4:11-14).

Watch out for yielding to the flesh. The natural man makes decisions out of sympathy or cunning or externals – and has ruined most everything we see around us that wears Jesus' Name. Most of the falls of major religious movements can be directly or indirectly traced back to this one point: allowing leadership (visible positions, "staff," or anyone "over" any area) that is less than full of the Holy Spirit and full of Wisdom.

Men have told me in more than one city that while they acknowledge that all of this is true, "Whatever would happen to the church if everyone who was not 'brimming with the power of God, full of the Holy Spirit,' stepped down from leadership? No one would be left!"

And I say to you, as I said to them: "That's not your concern. You obey God! And leave the rest to Him. *'Unless the Lord builds the House, it's builders build in vain.'* NEVER consider ramifications as you view the Word of God. Just OBEY GOD. It's His House, He can handle it. To disobey God in order to do Him a favor in His Church is to invite disaster." Please continue evermore to "walk by faith and not by sight."

Now that we know what kind of man should be regarded as a "leader," what do they do?   "Business Meetings," "Counselling Sessions," "Budgeting," "Office Management," and "Speech-Making" are *out.* These things are in *no way* related to the work of a man of God. A quick double-check of the Bible confirms the fact that these are not God's "job descriptions" for any of His men or women. Consider, though, how paralyzed today's religious organizations would be without these things. Bedlam. Or a total standstill.

So what do men and women "full of the Holy Spirit and Wisdom" look like in their daily lives and in gatherings of God's lambs? The answer might sound a little elusive, but anything else will cause the ambitious to attempt to carbon-copy something. And it will cause the fearful to shrink back. The critical, if given a "job description" would endanger their fellowship with God and His Church.   This, then, is really no cop-out at all: you'll definitely recognize the true nature of "leadership" when you personally encounter these Gifts from Heaven.

(In the mean time, you can get a pretty good idea about the substance of Divine Life in men and women by reading about the lives of Paul, Peter, Stephen, Philip, and the others. And read what these men of God wrote so that you can see how a man near God writes and acts. The Wisdom. The Intensity. The Depth. The Simplicity. The Fullness.) Pray to the Lord of the Harvest to send and raise up such laborers!

So what shall we do if no such men exist in the Family you are with? As scary and un-glorious as it may sound, just be brothers (Mat.23:8-11). Don't be like the Israelites who rejected God by wanting a king "like the other nations" – and hire someone to be the big cheese and spiritual giant. God forbid. Cry out together to the Lord of the Harvest to send or raise up laborers. Or, as God directs, move somewhere where you can "be equipped for works of ministry" (See Eph.4:9-16). But, whatever you do, heed not P. T. Barnum's (or whoever it was) advice often incorporated into "church": "THE SHOW MUST GO ON!" Simply gather to love one another, and to pray and fast and give glory to God, together. Please, don't just give in to the normal desire to put together a competitive SHOW, "like the other denomi-nations." Demolish the hierarchy (someone being in charge of teaching a "class" or running a "program"). These are based on human wisdom rather than on the Word of God. According to James, such a "wisdom" is "unspiritual, and of the devil."[79]

How refreshing, and ultimately fruitful, it will be to discard the Babylonian attempts to build towers to Heaven. Oh, for the end of the muck and mire and programs and politics. Oh! To see once again the very face of God. Amen.

---

[79] Proverbs 14:12, 16:25; James 3:15; Galatians 3:3.

Chapter Twenty-Seven

Important Encouragements

ALL that has been said so far, as you can see, does not have to do with meetings, per se, as much as it has to do with a way of Life. I want you to see a way of living for Christ that obliterates the shadows and lukewarmness in our own personal lives, and *then* ultimately in gatherings.

It's not our "Kingdom" – it's His. King Jesus reserves the right to run His Kingdom. And He's not running it by "absentee vote" via man's contradictory interpretations of a Book that He has written.

"As many as are led by the Spirit are Sons of God."

In context: "Creation itself GROANS in eager anticipation for the Sons of God to be manifested!" The two verses couldn't be more connected!

As for the "little things" that have everything to do with our potential and capacity for the future? Get practical! Christianity, as manifested in the Son, could not have been more tangible and practical! For starters, please get out of your rooms and homes, each of you, and consider who you can jump over and see. "Where is God's Action tonight?!" Do not keep to yourself, your hobbies – or television. (I know that you surely do not waste God's time in this way, with such self-indulgence, but, *believe it or not*, there will be some who may eventually happen across these chronicles who will still be enslaved or engrossed in such banal and wasteful things as television.)

Go! Go! Go! *Force* your way into a productive life for Christ Jesus (Mat.11:12). Be DEVOTED, "lay siege," to fellowship, and to the breaking of bread, and to the apostles' teaching, and to prayer (Acts 2:42). Go out and "forcefully enter the Kingdom." Beat down people's doors;[80] just get out there and do it. Again, *please* don't (if you are reading this and have been unknowingly sucked into the world system) vegetate in front of a mental pacifier, the trojan horse of a television set, or anything else you may have replaced it with. If it's bad seed you're sowing, don't kid yourself, "Be not deceived, God is not mocked;" you'll pay the price. Somebody said, in the Kingdom, "payday doesn't always come on Friday, but it always comes." If you spend your time *in any other way* than sowing good seed, even if it's just "neutral" seed, you'll pay the price eventually. (Farmers who don't sow seed know that they get weeds for free.) You'll be left in the dust of the people who have decided to "pull out the stops."

Conclusion: Let's make a difference on this earth before we leave it! I hope you're all committed to that task and are not willing to leave this planet without considerable evidence that you have been here. It's the will of the Father. *"This is to the Father's glory, that you bear much fruit . . . fruit that will last"* (John 15). It's to the Father's glory. It is His idea that we bear much fruit, fruit that will last. It's to His glory and it makes a difference. He cares whether we build with gold, silver, and precious stones that last and that will be refined, or whether we build with wood, hay and stubble which will be burnt up (1Cor.3:9-15). He cares. He wants us to make a difference on the earth. *"Come follow me,"* He said. *"I'll make you fishers of men."* And the Father is still calling out to us: "You will change men's destinies. You'll change everything around you just like my Son did, because the same Spirit who lived in Him and rose Him from the dead now lives in you. A man who is filled with the Spirit of Jesus, *will* make a difference. If a woman is filled and brimming with the Spirit of Jesus, she will bear much fruit – fruit that will last." Let's make a difference on this earth before we leave it. We don't want to be "some neat church." We want to tear down the gates of hell and break satan's back. Jesus said we could, and He wants us to in a very real and practical way. Let's be a Holy Nation, a people, a "vast army" (Ezek. 37) for Him. Go after it!

---

[80] Not just "hanging out" at someone's house making small talk and calling that "encouraging one another." Not a "christian fat farm" (1Tim.5:13) – but a place where warfare with the Enemy is waged, and we "strengthen one another's hand in God."

And the People of God said . . . "AMEN!"

By All Means RUN!

As each day passes by, there is always a need,
But temptation to drift is a real one indeed.
      My ears want to dull and my flesh gets its way,
      I need to press through, Lord, to hear what You say.

My eyes want to lower and focus on me,
My heart cries aloud, "Help me see what You see".
      I know that is not how You want me to be,
      I'm humbled and thankful, You always show me.

Thank You for showing me where I have been,
You're faithful to increase my hunger within.
      Your graciousness, Lord, helps me see You're the Source,
      With Your unending love, wipe away all remorse.

Your plan is not for Your sheep to give in,
But to rise above flesh and crucify sin.
      We may be prone to fall short of the mark,
      But life spent in neutral is life in the dark.

We're easily blinded and quite often fooled,
But by Your Son and Your Spirit, we've been well schooled.
      When we make the decisions and ourselves the boss,
      We've lost sight of You, and suffer great loss.

Let us be challenged, oh sinner and saint,
Lest we justify sin, and make ourselves great.
      We must see what He sees, and keep ourselves pure,
      With our purpose refined, and our hearts reassured.

Life is so short, and there's much to be done,
Keep your eyes set above, and by all means RUN!

Doug

Chapter Twenty-Eight

The City Church

(John 10:16)
"And other sheep I have which are not of this fold; them also I must bring, and they will hear My voice; and there will be one flock and one shepherd."

I T is not hard to establish in the Bible that God's Desire seems to be that there be but one Church in any given city.[81] Not one on every street corner.[82] Nowhere in the Scriptures does more than one "local church government" exist in any given city. While I could develop this point Biblically, I am much more inclined to ask you, "What would Jesus, our Messiah, desire? Separation? Division? Ambition? A contradictory Testimony to the community?" I think, in our hearts, we know the damage that has been done by the little parallel "kingdoms."

God said clearly that the way all men would know that we are His, is by visible, supernatural love that we exhibit towards one another. Now, doesn't it seem silly that each of us would be earnestly desiring to do God's Will and yet be living in an environment in our cities that contradicts the "*this* is how all men will know"?[83]

---

[81] I'm not referring even to several churches in a city that are <u>theoretically</u> "one" because the Ministers or Elders all get together regularly. ONE church. Really!

[82] Ezekiel 16:25.

[83] John 13:34-35.

Now, I realize that, although some of these groups that we find on the different street corners were indeed started out of ambition or division ("We're the only ones with pure doctrine," etc.), others were genuine in their desire to do God's Will. They longed to serve Him together in a higher way than would be tolerated by the moribund religious group that they had left. Others have begun "additional churches" in a city because they simply desired to obey the "Great Commission" (and felt as if other groups in the city were not doing a satisfactory job of the work).

After we agree with God that Oneness is His desire and we commit to obey Him in tearing down obstacles of fear, sin, pride, ambition, and prejudice, there still is a large obstacle to "one church per city." The obstacle is this: We can't simply subject ourselves to the "lowest common denominator" approach. We cannot just say: "Everyone who calls themselves a christian . . . we'll all be one from now on." To accept things that Jesus does not accept is to deny His Lordship.

(Jeremiah 23:18-22)
"But which of them has stood in the council of the Lord to see or to hear his word? Who has listened and heard his word? See, the storm of the Lord will burst out in wrath, a whirlwind swirling down on the heads of the wicked. The anger of the Lord will not turn back until he fully accomplishes the purposes of his heart. In days to come you will understand it clearly. I did not send these prophets, yet they have run with their message; I did not speak to them, yet they have prophesied. But if they had stood in my council, they would have proclaimed my words to my people and would have turned them from their evil ways and from their evil deeds."

(Lamentations 2:14)
"The visions of your prophets were false and worthless; they did not expose your sin to ward off your captivity. The oracles they gave you were false and misleading."

(2Corinthians 6:14-18)
What do righteousness and wickedness have in common? Or what fellowship can light have with darkness? . . .
As God has said: "I will live with them and walk among them, and I will be their God, and they will be my people. Therefore come out from them and be separate," says the Lord. "Touch no unclean thing,

and I will receive you. I will be a Father to you, and you will be my sons and daughters," says the Lord Almighty.

It is abundantly clear that it is not God's desire to have **compromise** be the ingredient that we all submit to in order to "unite" His People. No! If not compromise, then what *will* draw His Holy Nation, all of His People, into the Testimony of Oneness to which He has called us, in every city and around the world? How will a glorious, beautiful church that "has made herself ready for the Return of Christ" emerge from the rubble of the fragmented mixture that wears our Lord's Name in most every city?

It was the passion of our King and Brother, Jesus, to see all of His People ONE in the midst of "all men" – our communities. Do His Zeal and Priorities really live within us and consume us that we have the same passionate desire as Jesus to be ONE?

How could it ever happen that we could unite? If not compromise, then what?!

Jesus answered . . . and demonstrated the answer.

(John 17:20-23)
"I pray also for those who will believe in me through their message, that all of them may be one, Father, just as you are in me and I am in you. May they also be in us so that the world may believe that you have sent me. I have given them the Glory that you gave me, that they may be one as we are one: I in them and you in me. May they be brought to complete unity to let the world know that you sent me and have loved them even as you have loved me."

We cannot possibly unite on the basis of the "lowest common denominator" approach. Yet that Oneness that God desires will be possible as we see God pouring out His Glory once again. His Glory will melt the fears and the misgivings and misunderstandings. God pouring out His Glory once again will cause those that love the dark mist of self-will and self-indulgence to flee (John 3:19-21). *"Like Jannes and Jambres . . . their folly will be evident to all."*

He'll deluge us with His Shekinah Glory and bring us to a unity that is visible, rather than imaginary. Not just a "worldly" religious counterfeit of Glory for which the wicked and adulterous generations drool. The world will see His Glory in the Agape that is expressed in our surrender to the Cross for others (John 13:34-35). We'll see His Glory displayed also in the presents of His Presence (Eph.4:11-13). As before, He will manifest His Love and Compassion amongst the poor.

And we'll be one. Like . . .

Two called "apostles" that, prior to meeting Jesus, had insurmountable differences:

Matthew: the repulsive "tax collector" – considered a "Benedict Arnold" by his Jewish countrymen. He collected Roman taxes and extorted money from his own people as an occupation.

Simon "the Zealot": revolutionary Jew, bent on vengeance towards the Romans and their puppets – such as the "tax collectors."

In principle, two sworn enemies. Standing before Jesus, the Christ, those differences didn't really seem to matter much. There is no record of Matthew and Simon reaching any political detente. It was just that something much bigger than their finite minds could contain was now enveloping them and then melting them together. The full expanse of the Love of God was shining on them *together*. The radiance of God was now shining "the light of the knowledge of the Glory of God in the face of Christ." All questions were answered in the manifestation and personification of Truth and Love: Jesus Christ, "who has become for us wisdom from God – that is, our righteousness, holiness and redemption." Jesus is "the power of God and the wisdom of God." When we've truly met Jesus, the Anointed One of God, foolishness melts, wounds are made whole, and darkness is exposed and driven out. And we are made One. May God pour out His Glory once again for the sake of His Beloved Son.

The Father brought Oneness in Caesarea, not by debate or compromise, but by His Glory (Acts 10:1-11:18, 11:17). He brought Oneness in the face of tremendous doctrinal difficulties, not by perpetual argumentation, but by the testimony of His Glory revealed (Acts 15:12).

In our day, it will require all three of these things to see God's Purposes (in making us as One Body, to demonstrate His Love and Power) accomplished:

1. A clear vision[84] of what The Christ of God desires in making us One New Man in life, as well as in concept. We must *forbear* our external distinctions.

(Colossians 3:11-14)
   "there is neither Greek nor Jew, circumcised nor uncircumcised, barbarian, Scythian, slave nor free, but Christ is all and in all. Therefore, as the elect of God, holy and beloved, put on tender mercies, kindness, humbleness of mind, meekness, longsuffering; bearing with one another, and forgiving one another, if anyone has a complaint against another; even as Christ forgave you, so you also must do. But above all these things put on love, which is the bond of perfection."

(Ephesians 4:1-6)
   "I, therefore, the prisoner of the Lord, beseech you to have a walk worthy of the calling with which you were called, with all lowliness and gentleness, with longsuffering, bearing with one another in love, endeavoring to keep the unity of the Spirit in the bond of peace. There is one body and one Spirit, just as you were called in one hope of your calling; one Lord, one faith, one baptism; one God and Father of all, who is above all, and through all, and in you all."

2. And the willingness to live in the Light together – the Light of exposure and humility and holiness (John 3:19-21; 2Thes.2:10-12; John 10:4-5). We can never have true fellowship with one another and "Him who is from the Beginning" as long as sin remains hidden in our closets, and defensiveness, fear, and distance (hypocrisy) remain between us:

(1John 1:5-7)
   "This is the message which we have heard from Him and declare to you, that God is light and in Him is no darkness at all. If we say that we have fellowship with Him, and walk in darkness, we lie and do not

---

[84] Proverbs 29:18.

practice the truth. But if we walk in the light as He is in the light, we have fellowship with one another, and the blood of Jesus Christ His Son cleanses us from all sin."

There must be the confession of, and the dealing with, sin in our assemblies. Not just some great "worship time" and skirting the real issues. Not just "preaching sermons" about it, hoping that the guilty will straighten up. Real dealing with it! With people, *by name*, as Jesus and Paul and John did. If we will not do this, the rest is, according to God, hopeless.

(1 Corinthians 5:6-13)
> *"Your glorying is not good. **Do you not know that a little leaven leavens the whole lump?** Therefore purge out the old leaven, that you may be a new lump, since you truly are unleavened. For indeed Christ, our Passover, was sacrificed for us. Therefore let us keep the feast, not with old leaven, nor with the leaven of malice and wickedness, but with the unleavened bread of sincerity and truth.*
> *"I wrote to you in my epistle not to keep company with sexually immoral people. Yet I certainly did not mean with the sexually immoral people of this world, or with the covetous, or extortioners, or idolaters, since then you would need to go out of the world.*
> *"But now I have written to you not to keep company with anyone **who calls himself a brother**, who is sexually immoral, or covetous, or an idolater ['devoted to any object or hobby or pursuit that has more sway in one's life than seeking God's Kingdom and Purposes day to day'], or a reviler ['foul tongue, railing, abusive, slandering'], or a drunkard, or an extortioner – not even to eat with such a person.*
> *"For what have I to do with judging those also who are outside? Do you not judge those who are **inside**? But those who are outside God judges. Therefore put away from yourselves that wicked person."*

As another example (if that is even necessary after such clear teaching from God):

(Joshua 7:4-6, 10-15)
> *So about three thousand men went up there from the people, but they fled before the men of Ai. And the men of Ai struck down about thirty six men, for they chased them from before the gate as far as Shebarim, and struck them down on the descent; therefore the hearts of the people melted and became like water.*

Then Joshua tore his clothes, and fell to the earth on his face before the ark of the Lord until evening, both he and the elders of Israel; and they put dust on their heads.

So the Lord said to Joshua: "Get up! Why do you lie thus on your face? Israel has sinned, and they have also transgressed My covenant which I commanded them. For they have even taken some of the accursed things, and have both stolen and deceived; and they have also put it among their own stuff.

"Therefore the children of Israel could not stand before their enemies, but turned their backs before their enemies, because they have become doomed to destruction. Neither will I be with you anymore, unless you destroy the accursed from among you. Get up, sanctify the people, and say, 'Sanctify yourselves for tomorrow, because thus says the Lord God of Israel: There is an accursed thing in your midst, O Israel; you cannot stand before your enemies until you take away the idol from among you.

'In the morning therefore you shall be brought according to your tribes. And it shall be that the tribe which the Lord takes shall come according to families; and the family which the Lord takes shall come by households; and the household which the Lord takes shall come man by man. Then it shall be that he who is taken with the accursed thing shall be burned with fire, he and all that he has, because he has transgressed the covenant of the Lord, and because he has done a disgraceful thing in Israel.'"

God's People were bent on victory – but God allowed them to be crushed by inferior adversaries because of hidden sin "in the Church." No matter what other good things we might do, we can not prosper in our desire to possess God's Promises as long as we allow idols to be hidden inside the camp.

Now I'll grant you that in the majority of religious organizations today it is not practical or even possible to obey God and "get the leaven out of the batch" without a legalistic witch hunt, probably executed by the worst of the lot. In a "certain time at a certain place" kind of religious body, error-prone, hypocritical legalism is the only alternative to the normal practice (blatant disobedience to God's Command to "get the leaven out of the batch"). Unfortunately, in a faulty religious institutional environment, we'll tend to cut off the weak and keep the impostors.

But guess what?! When His Church is again an "organism," rather than an "organization," it is amazing how effective God's Ways are! Do you realize the power and depth of relationship that men and women had in the early church? Even the weakest congregation of the Church of Jesus in the Bible had something that most of today's world hasn't come anywhere near to experiencing. Today in the churches "more sophisticated" than Corinth, such a thing as refusing to eat with a man would be scoffed at, and would be totally ineffective even if it were carried out as God said. Yet even in a weak church (built on the *right* Foundation) the relationships were so deep that just this refusal of God's People to *eat* with a man drove him to his knees, and back to God.[85] Would that happen where you are? I really want it to be so, and I know that you do, too. And, of course, it would please our Father very much if His children were so close to one another.

How *would* you describe the depth and reality of your corporate Life? Are you all truly are "joined and knit together by every supporting ligament?" If not, you can never be the Testimony of Jesus on earth that He means you to be. You'll be handcuffed. We can never show the world that we are His disciples without showing them how we love one another. Jesus is still saying: "THIS is how all men will know . . . ." And without that depth of relationship that allows us to get intimately involved with one another's struggles, we can never obey God and, in love, "get the leaven out of the batch." If we cannot deal with the leaven, according to God Himself, we will *all* be leavened and the batch (church) ruined because the leaven remains.

God's principle from the Garden to Eternity (Genesis 3:23; Rev.21:27) and everywhere in between (Numbers 25:6-13, Psa.106:28-31; 1Cor.5:6-13; 2Cor.6:17) is the same: "Do you not know that a little leaven leavens the whole lump? Get the leaven out of the batch." You'll not be able to bypass this point and know God's Life.[86]

---

[85] 1Corinthians 5:6-13, 2Corinthians 2:6-8, 7:8-11.

[86] Because this is such a widespread difficulty for people, I'll make a point (for those who are wondering) about Matthew 13:24-43, the Parable of the Wheat and the Tares (weeds). Someone started the rumor that because of this parable, 1Cor.5:6-13 mustn't be obeyed. This is a huge problem. For us to call ourselves Christians and

The Life of our Lord, our "Pioneer," is described by the Father this way:

(Hebrews 1:9)
"You have loved righteousness and hated wickedness; therefore God, your God, has set you above your companions by anointing you with the oil of joy."

What is the "therefore" referring to? **Why** did God anoint Jesus? Because He "loved righteousness and hated wickedness." You live that way too, OK? Join your Lord!

3. **And, beyond all of that, the Father will answer the prayer of His Beloved Son and fuse us together: By the GLORY of God revealed! Nothing in Heaven or on earth can bring us together, truly, short of God's GLORY being poured out over the face of the earth. And He will do it. Jesus doesn't have unanswered prayers. Amen.**

---

not obey God is a contradiction to the extreme! "If you love me, you'll keep my commandments." We must obey 1Cor.5, which commands us to remove those who will not bow their knee to Jesus, in their every day lives, from the church. There are no choices.

So how does the parable of the wheat and the tares fit in? First, check your motives for not wanting to get leaven out of the batch. (Are you that leaven? Or, are you fearful to deal with others because you "love the praise of men more than the praise of God" and don't want people to get upset with you?) Second, the "field" in which the weeds (that we cannot uproot) are sown is **not** "the Church." According to Jesus, "the field is the WORLD," **not** the Church (verse 38). In other words, it is not a "social utopia" on planet earth that we are after. The "enemy" has sown weeds on God's earth in order to choke God's Sons (Mat.13:22) and make them unfruitful. The "field" that we cannot remove all of the weeds from until the "end of the age" is, according to Jesus, "the WORLD." Not the Church. "IN the world, but not OF it." In the Church, we MUST do what God commanded and "get the leaven out of the batch." We are not His Church if we will not do what He says (John 14:15; Acts 3:23; Rev.2:5, 3:16).

(James 4:4)
"Adulterers and adulteresses! Do you not know that friendship with the **world** is enmity with God? Whoever therefore wants to be a friend of the **world** makes himself an **enemy** of God."

"I have given them the Glory that you gave me, that they may be one as we are one: I in them and you in me. May they be brought to complete unity to let the world know that you sent me and have loved them even as you have loved me."

Live for the pouring out of that Glory once again. Live for the day that God tears down the walls in the *Denomi*-nations in the same astounding "overnight" way as the walls of the *nations* have crumbled in the eastern bloc in the past few months (1989, 1990)! As the immovable Berlin Wall was dismantled virtually overnight . . . as the day of Pentecost brought masses of dozens of nations together under one Head in but a few minutes . . . so also will God destroy the dividing walls amongst those who seek Him with pure hearts. Live for the day that in every city the Testimony would be clear: "When you've seen Gary, you've seen me." "When you've seen Linda, you've seen me." One church, if even with mega-thousands, in a locale. No more franchises of someone's dream, genius, and flair. Unless it is that of Jesus alone!

Dare we settle for anything less than the heart-cry of our Messiah? Forget the details and the "practical issues" – God will just have to show us how to work them out. But **we'll not lower the call of God in order to accommodate our lack of wisdom about "how"** it **could be.** Sons of Abraham have the heart of Abraham when it comes to facing the "impossible":

(Romans 4:17-21)
"Abraham is our father in the sight of God, in whom he believed – the God who gives life to the dead and calls things that are not as though they were. Against all hope, Abraham in hope believed and so became the father of many nations, just as it had been said to him, 'So shall your offspring be.'

"Without weakening in his faith, he faced the fact that his body was as good as dead – since he was about a hundred years old – and that Sarah's womb was also dead. Yet he did not waver through unbelief regarding the promise of God, but was strengthened in his faith and gave glory to God, being fully persuaded that God had power to do what he had promised."

How badly do you want what God wants – a Testimony of Oneness in your city? Please don't see all of this as an "optional extra" – like the monogram of your initials on your Bible. "That's nice for you, if you want to do that." Value to the point of death what God prizes, what Jesus fervently prayed for, and what He was willing to die for. Once again the "dividing wall of hostility" must come down! Is anything else "Christian?"

Chapter Twenty-Nine

"What It Ain't"

N OW, envision 17,000 or more as part of one church, *the* church of Christ Jesus in a city. How would they still allow the Lord of Hosts to be Head of His Church? Would it now have to revert (in the "daily in public" part of "daily in public and from house to house") to a slick Hi-Tech Hollywood presentation by some well-groomed marketeers and choreographers? Would the show need to be planned out step-by-step and practiced again and again all week long, in order to "get it right" on the big day? Is that New Testament Christianity? You know better.[87] Paul would have blown a cork if such a thing were even suggested! John would have wept aloud . . . just before, as a true "Son of Thunder," he tore into the stage props and troupes. What great lengths we have gone to in our day to fill in the vacuum left by Ichabod, the departure of true Glory. We have discovered, as in Jesus' day, that, in spite of the ongoing religious ceremonies, the Ark is not in the Temple.

I must add two things at this point:

1.   While this may seem "negative," keep in mind that severe problems require an accurate diagnosis. Otherwise we'll never have the heart and passion to find the cure. And,

---

[87] God is after "skilled" from Above (Ex.35:31, 36:1) men and women. These are so adept at what they do that "the eyes of their hearts" can be fully turned towards the Captain of the Lord's Host as they do what they do with their "skills." They are then able to respond to the variables and God's Direction with a great amount of "Spontaneity." Some need to concentrate on the mechanics of what they are doing because they have only a limited level of giftedness. They cannot look full into Jesus' Face and forget about everything external. Those that cannot so lose themselves in Christ while they do what they are doing cannot lead others into His Presence in that area. "Practicing" or "Studying" something is not the issue. Practicing to learn, or to enhance a skill, is commendable, but never to fulfill a little pre-programmed role. Do what you do to change who you **are** before God: to grow into His Image, and to offer yourself to Him. But not to perform a clever ditty before men. Get who you **are** right, and He'll use you as He sees fit! "Unless the Lord builds the House, its builders build in vain."

2.   We don't have to stay in this state of
          affairs unless we prefer it, for reasons of
          our own!

I don't really need to describe any more of what is happening today. You've seen it. Suffice it to say that while God, for the most part, may have appreciated our sincerity, most of the fruit of being disconnected from the Head has been tragic. The divorce rate is as high in the "churches" as in the world. Teenage girls are getting pregnant left and right. Drinking, drugs, vulgarity, and worldliness of every kind are filling up pews on Sunday morning all over the world – and "God is not amused." Might we at least *consider* the fact that this tragic stuff wouldn't be going on unchecked if Jesus were *really* (rather than just theoretically) Present in His Church?

(Matthew 16:18)
  "I will build my Church . . . and the gates of Hell (the powers of the infernal region) shall not overpower it (or be strong to its detriment or hold out against it)."

(1John 3:7-10)
  *"Dear children, **do not let anyone lead you astray.** He who does what is right is righteous, just as he is righteous. He who does what is sinful is of the devil, because the devil has been sinning from the beginning.*
  *"**The reason the Son of God appeared was to destroy the works of the devil:** No one who is born of God will continue to sin, because God's seed remains in him; he cannot go on sinning, because he has been born of God. This is how we know who the children of God are and who the children of the devil are: Anyone who does not do what is right is not a child of God; nor is anyone who does not love his brother."*

Chapter Thirty

Jesus' Headship in Large Family Gatherings

"And all the believers used to meet together in Solomon's Colonnade."

C ONSIDER now the "more than we can ask or imagine" possibility of hundreds, or thousands, of true Christians (followers and true personal friends of Jesus of Nazareth: resurrected, exalted King) under one local church government.[88] One church in the city, as it was in the first century (and would surely please Him at His Coming) – the church that has "made herself ready for the Return of the Groom."[89]

Keep in mind that this kind of church can only ever be seen if built on the Foundation properly laid (1Cor.3:9-15)[90] by those "master-builders" qualified to lay such a Foundation in a city (unless God chooses to overshadow the "normal" means of bringing such a

---

[88] Hebrews 13:17 – everyone called Christian should know "who has the rule over them," who "watches over them," and who "must give an account" for them. If you do not, then you are almost certainly outside of God's Will for your life. I know that many have abused this and every other Truth imaginable. Nevertheless, only a rebel or a fool would throw out Scripture because someone somewhere abused it and started a movement around their abuse. You do what you need to do! Know who the men of God are who "have the rule over you" in the context of the local church that you must be a part of to find God's highest favor. "The hand cannot say to the eye: 'I have no need of you.'"

[89] Due to the immense confusion that the enemy has created in trying to prejudice God's Saints from the Truth by perverting the Word of God, I need to say this again. I am **not** referring to a church that has created a social utopia. Rather, as demonstrated in the Spirit as the "Suffering Servant," I am crying out for a church walking in the true Power and Love and Holiness of God – totally obscured to the carnal eye by the "no beauty or majesty" garments of their Lord.

[90] Apostolic Foundations and Apostolic Patterns.

thing about – Eph.4:11-17). Without this kind of Foundation, we'll find ourselves trying desperately to mimic something that we don't even understand. It won't work. Cry out to the Lord of the Harvest!

What does "Church" look like when multitudes are part of a single church in a city? The evidence is strong from the chronicles of the early Church by Dr. Luke, as well as the letters from Paul to the Corinthians and others, and the excavations of Antioch and other early cities where Jesus manifested Himself (John 14:12-31, 14:19) in His Church.[91] I'll give you a partial picture based on this evidence.

The church consisted of Believers often living very near each other (though not "communal" – Acts 5:1,4 – their land and possessions still belonged to them, and they gave as they did because of their relationship with God). They were totally involved in each other's lives (in response to the simple teaching and Spirit of Christ in them), daily, from house to house, and in the gathering together of the entire church in the city on a frequent basis. Christians circled around a number of different homes on a daily basis. The entire church was together frequently from all parts of the city. Also, continual public teaching often went on in a neutral place like a rented hall.[92]

---

[91] In addition to the Biblical, historical, and archaeological findings, we can have some idea of what happened then by what is happening now. "By its fruit ye shall know it." Quite a lot of what we see journaled in the Bible can only be understood from the "inside looking out." Jesus said, "If anyone wants to **do** His will, he shall know concerning the teaching, whether it is from God or whether I speak on My own authority." And, John wrote, "The **LIFE** becomes the Light of men." It is only in **doing** that we can know what the Bible is talking about. If our religious groups are totally foreign to the church of the Bible in commitment and practice, those involved can never "study" hard enough to understand what "Church" is really all about. The modern "definitions" given to the teachings of the Bible will obscure and dilute what really happened and what God really meant to have as a Bride, an equal yoke, for His Son.

[92] Acts 19:8; Acts 19:9-10; Acts 18:19; Acts 18:26-28; Acts 17:16-17; This public location was **not** "the church," but where men and women from all over the city and the world were taught **about** the church. The church is people. If you can "attend" it, it absolutely is not the Church that Jesus started.

A number of different homes became recognized as "the place to be," the evening's starting place, the "default" place to begin searching for the adoration of God by gathered saints, or the "equipping for works of service," or the "sending out" place on any given night. Those who were found there might have all ended up going two by two into the urban jungle to "sustain the weary." Or they might have wrestled in prayer all night together. They might often find themselves together with an unbeliever who someone had brought over, and spend the evening introducing him or her to our Jesus. If the entire church was not gathering that day or evening, there was always going to be some action, depending on where you lived. At Acquila and Priscilla's house. And Philemon's. Paul's rented house in Rome. Maybe the homes of Aristobulus and Chloe. The home of Nymphas was an "eye of the storm" of God's Whirlwind of Power in that city. Peter knew just where to go to find a bunch of Christians, even at a late hour![93] They gathered continually "from house to house," and even seemed to purposely live in clusters in a city such as Antioch (population circa 500,000).

What were gatherings like in those times when the one church in Jerusalem gathered in one place? We've already spoken of the "from house to house" gatherings in great detail. But what happened when thousands of truly converted disciples of Jesus gathered together daily[94] "publicly" in the Jerusalem city park (a semi-covered promenade area known as Solomon's Porch, or Solomon's Colonnade)? You *know*, from the Life of Jesus, the record

---

[93] Acts 12:1-17. Were James and others gathering elsewhere?

[94] We know that, at times, they did meet as a whole Church, daily (Acts 2:42-47, 4:32-35; Heb.3:13; Mark 8:34-9:1). What does that say, for starters, about the focus of their lives? Did they "have to" meet every day? In what Scripture would "daily gatherings" have been mandated? They wanted to! Even as "baby Christians" their lives belonged fully to Him. That was (and is) the very nature of becoming a Christian, "confessing Him as Lord" (Rom.10:9-10)! Do you want to be where Jesus is "in the midst" - where His Saints are "gathered," or are you looking for a loophole and getting upset or defensive? This is a good test of who your Lord really is. How'd you do?! (Sometimes a real church in a city may not meet, as a whole, every day. That's certainly OK. But what if it is meeting that often? What is your attitude? And if the entire church isn't together every night, what do you long to do with your evening instead? Are you "seeking first the Kingdom" every night anyway? As I said, this is a good test of who you really are. "What we treasure is where our hearts are.")

of the Bible, and the pure principles of God and the Church of His Son, that it was (and is *still*) un-programmed communion with the Head of the Church.[95]

One thing that will be a little different in the mega-gatherings is that, unlike most of the action that takes place "from house to house," a few men will tend to be more visible than the rest. *Though no one is ever assigned to be the "leader" of any particular event or gathering, large or small, in the church of the Bible,* some gifts do definitely stand out more prominently than others.

(Acts 2:41-47)
   "Those who accepted his message were baptized, and about three thousand were added to their number that day. They devoted themselves to the apostles' teaching and to the fellowship, to the breaking of bread and to prayer. Everyone was filled with awe, and many wonders and miraculous signs were done by the apostles. All the believers were together and had everything in common. Selling their possessions and goods, they gave to anyone as he had need. Every day they continued to meet together in the temple courts (city park). They broke bread in their homes and ate together with glad and sincere hearts, praising God and enjoying the favor of all the people. And the Lord added to their number daily those who were being saved."

(Acts 4:2)
   "They were greatly disturbed because the apostles were teaching the people and proclaiming in Jesus the resurrection of the dead."

(Acts 4:33)
   "With great power the apostles continued to testify to the resurrection of the Lord Jesus, and mega-grace was upon them all."

---

[95] Do you want to know how the day of Pentecost could have been thoroughly ruined and robbed of the Life-giving power that was poured out? One sure-fire way to have grieved the Spirit of God right out of the city would have been to have distributed flyers around the city that said: "Come Hear Peter Expound on Joel, Chapter Two!"
   As ridiculous as that may sound to you (hopefully), today we do such things regularly, and expect that God will endorse these activities.

The apostles, the "sent-from-God-ones," had a very visible role in the "whole church" gatherings. Was that because they were paid to "preach" and they took turns delivering the "sermons" on Sunday morning? Wrong-ola. There were no men "paid to preach,"[96] and there were no "sermons" as we have come to know them. And, no, the apostles did not "take turns." If any of that was the case, it would have flagrantly contradicted the life and the teaching of Jesus. The whole nature of the Church that they were celebrating together would have been debased by any such Ishmaelic practices.[97] They were not going to return to the Old Covenant "basic principles of this world" way of life after rubbing elbows for three years with the Carpenter, "the Eternal Life" (1John 1:1-7).

We know that those who knew Jesus best were those who everyone wanted to be equipped by. Those who could part the Heavens and draw the hands of His Children up to meet the Hands of Jesus were the ones who were most visible in the large gatherings. I'm not speaking of hirelings or "staff members," but those who were *living* in "the Power of an Indestructible Life," "Tasting the Powers of the Coming Age," "Rivers of Living Water Gushing from their bellies," with a true current fellowship with "Him Who is from the Beginning" – and could draw and equip them into that same inheritance, meant to be theirs from before time. There was (Acts 2:42-45), and is, a holy Awe when men who know Him, men with an "open Heaven," pour out the New Wine on God's People.

Who taught? It all depended. *"If a revelation comes to someone who is sitting down, the first one speaking should stop."* (Not the "man of the hour." Jesus alone held that position – Mat.23:8-10). If we are still the followers of a living Lord, a living Head of the Church,

---

[96] Servants of God who were bearing the fruit of the Anointed One were responded to organically (Gal.6:6), not in some salaried, white-collar way as a "peddlar of the Word of God." The response materially to those that emanated the Life and Power of their Lord was definitely there, but apparently not much like today's typical situation.

[97] Carrying out "God's Purposes" . . . by man mating God's Intention with a world-system "practicality" and "good ideas," rather than cleaving to the Spirit of God. A book entitled <u>The Church: Ishmael's Pew or Isaac's Glory</u> may be available in the future, as time and other resources allow.

nothing has changed. But it was *likely* to be one who had demonstrably walked in His Life and His Love. One who had been refined by His Priesthood – Living Stones rubbing against one another to rub off the sharp edges. One who had experienced, and now welcomes His discipline. One whose daily Life had clearly shattered darkness everywhere he had planted his feet. One who had borne the visible fruit of authority in the *unseen* world, of *"tearing down satan's strongholds"* in every arena of life into which he had ventured. It certainly had nothing whatsoever to do with education, eloquence, payroll, rotation, or even sincerity. It was determined by the Life from Heaven.[98]

It isn't that the center of attention *couldn't* have been a new Christian or an "unknown" at any given time. There was nothing in the bylaws and nothing in the "order of worship" that would disallow the possibility. Anyone *could* be at the forefront at a public time such as this (and, no doubt, this happened as God did special things), it's just that it wasn't usually *necessary* for anyone else to say a whole lot!

Consider another picture of a New Testament Church gathering:

(Acts 20:7-11)
"Now on the first day of the week, when the disciples came together to break bread, Paul, ready to depart the next day, reasoned with them and continued his expressions of God's Truth until midnight.
"There were many lamps in the upper room where they were gathered together. And in a window sat a certain young man named Eutychus, who was sinking into a deep sleep. He was overcome by sleep; and as Paul continued the discussion, he fell down from the third story

---

[98] If you've never witnessed or experienced such life, which most church attenders admittedly have not, then this will seem impossible and impractical to you. It's not! Your part?

"The kingdom of heaven is like treasure hidden in a field. When a man found it, he hid it again, and then in his joy went and sold all he had and bought that field.

"Again, the kingdom of heaven is like a merchant looking for fine pearls. When he found one of great value, he went away and sold everything he had and bought it."

and was taken up dead. But Paul went down, fell on him, and embracing him said, 'Do not trouble yourselves, for his life is in him.'

"Now when Paul had come up, had broken bread and eaten, and talked a long while, even till daybreak, he departed."

Did Paul "preach" a multiple-hour "sermon" from behind a "pulpit?" Not a chance. But was Paul the primary voice in the "dialogue" (as was said earlier, this is the Greek word) between the brothers? Definitely. Why did Paul do most of the teaching of God's Ways? Because he was hired to? No! Paul didn't "dominate" the brothers and sisters in Troas, or anywhere (2Cor.1:24; 1Thes.2:1-13; Mat.20:25-28). Anyone who had a Word from Heaven could bring it to God's Saints. It was not that no one else *could* be the one to supply God's Truth to the moment at hand. It was just that with a gifted, consecrated servant like Paul in the room, a lot of additional input from others was not usually necessary! This man knew God. Throwing opinions around with this man present would have been a) dangerous; b) a waste of precious time; and c) like fingernails on a chalkboard to everyone else in the room. Yet, if the Father had raised up another man of similar true Stature before God in their midst, or one had happened in from another place, it would have been double fun as these two men together elevated the gathering of the Saints to heights and riches unimaginable.

If we are really earnest and honest in wanting to know whether we are really letting Jesus be Head of the Church of which we are a part, an excellent test would be this:

Suppose Paul or John, or even Jesus Himself were to show up at the assembly (in blue jeans and a T-Shirt) that you are a part of. Would they "get a Word in edgewise?" Or would we so fully dominate the time with spiritual things (that we had prepared in advance to do) that we would entirely miss what *God* wanted to do? Possibly the entire time was supposed to be taught by the "visitor" that no one had known previously (with the visitor naturally working with any God-sent overseers, as is God's way). And, if God had His way, the gathering was to go on from 9 A.M. or so until dawn the next day.

Would that even be *possible* in the group of which you are a part?   If not, someone other than Jesus is the Head of the organization.

I really don't want to get into a "cookbook" approach to Jesus' church and give a recipe for the perfect "large gathering."   That's really the point: they'll all be different.   Some will be primarily serious teaching, others rowdy and joyous with praise to Y'shua. Practical instruction, prayer for those maimed by the enemy, some confession (usually as it relates to the broad scope of the whole church – the "house to house" times have already served most of these needs on a daily basis), vision and direction from God for the future through His servants, songs offered that were written by the saints, and many other kinds of things are likely to occur.   Most of the Glory of what *could* happen will only be understood from the perspective of observing it happen, rather than postulating and analyzing.   Better to do our part to see revival in our cities, and to trust God for Wisdom of how to handle it when it comes, than to second guess in advance.   The twelve hadn't any experience with a church of 3000 until the time came, either!

Chapter Thirty-One

"We Being MANY Are One Body"

"But in a large church we can't know everyone."

R EST assured, when everyone is truly built on that Foundation of a *Living* Christ, that apostolic Foundation of "obedience of the Faith," that "Rock" of Surrender,[99] the church of mega-thousands will be ONE, from end to end. *"From the least, to the greatest, they shall all know me."*

It can be likened to a piece of cloth four miles on a side. Is every thread directly adjacent to every other thread? No. But every thread is part of the one fabric, and woven in and out in such a way that all are joined and one. While I may not be adjacent to every thread, I do touch every thread through the other threads. We **are** One, through the current Life and Spirit of Jesus.

(Romans 12:1-9)

"Therefore, I urge you, brothers, in view of God's mercy, to offer your bodies as living sacrifices, holy and pleasing to God - this is your spiritual act of worship. Do not conform any longer to the pattern of this world, but be transformed by the renewing of your mind. Then you will be able to test and approve what God's will is - his good, pleasing and perfect will.

"For by the grace given me I say to every one of you: Do not think of yourself more highly than you ought, but rather think of yourself with sober judgment, in accordance with the measure of faith God has given you. Just as each of us has one body with many members, and these members do not all have the same function, so in Christ we who are many form one body, and each member belongs to all the others.

"We have different gifts, according to the grace given us. If a man's gift is prophesying, let him use it in proportion to his faith. If it is serving, let him serve; if it is teaching, let him teach; if it is

---

[99] 1Cor.3:9-11; Rom.1:1-6; Eph.2:19-22, 4:11-13; Mat.7:13-29.

encouraging, let him encourage; if it is contributing to the needs of others, let him give generously; if it is leadership, let him govern diligently; if it is showing mercy, let him do it cheerfully. Love must be sincere. Hate what is evil; cling to what is good."

(1Corinthians 12:1-31)

"Now about spiritual gifts, brothers, I do not want you to be ignorant. You know that when you were pagans, somehow or other you were influenced and led astray to mute idols. Therefore I tell you that no one who is speaking by the Spirit of God says, "Jesus be cursed," and no one can say, "Jesus is Lord," except by the Holy Spirit.

"There are different kinds of gifts, but the same Spirit. There are different kinds of service, but the same Lord. There are different kinds of working, but the same God works all of them in all men. Now to each one the manifestation of the Spirit is given for the common good. To one there is given through the Spirit the message of wisdom, to another the message of knowledge by means of the same Spirit, to another faith by the same Spirit, to another gifts of healing by that one Spirit, to another miraculous powers, to another prophecy, to another distinguishing between spirits, to another speaking in different kinds of tongues, and to still another the interpretation of tongues. All these are the work of one and the same Spirit, and he gives them to each one, just as he determines.

"The body is a unit, though it is made up of many parts; and though all its parts are many, they form one body. So it is with Christ. For we were all baptized by one Spirit into one body - whether Jews or Greeks, slave or free - and we were all given the one Spirit to drink.

"Now the body is not made up of one part but of many. If the foot should say, 'Because I am not a hand, I do not belong to the body,' it would not for that reason cease to be part of the body. And if the ear should say, 'Because I am not an eye, I do not belong to the body,' it would not for that reason cease to be part of the body. If the whole body were an eye, where would the sense of hearing be? If the whole body were an ear, where would the sense of smell be? But in fact God has arranged the parts in the body, every one of them, just as he wanted them to be.

"If they were all one part, where would the body be? As it is, there are many parts, but one body. The eye cannot say to the hand, 'I don't need you!' And the head cannot say to the feet, 'I don't need you!' On the contrary, those parts of the body that seem to be weaker are indispensable, and the parts that we think are less honorable we treat with special honor. And the parts that are unpresentable are *treated with special modesty, while our presentable parts need no special treatment. But God has combined the members of the body and has given greater honor to the parts that lacked it, so that there should be no division in the body, but that its parts should have equal concern for each other. If one part suffers, every part suffers with it; if one part is honored, every part rejoices with it.*

"Now you are the body of Christ, and each one of you is a part of it. And in the church God has appointed first of all apostles, second prophets, third teachers, then workers of miracles, also those having gifts of healing, those able to help others, those with gifts of administration, and those speaking in different kinds of tongues. Are all apostles? Are all prophets? Are all teachers? Do all work miracles? Do all have gifts of healing? Do all speak in tongues ? Do all interpret? But eagerly desire the greater gifts."

The reality, the visible expression of this Truth, is very special. If we are truly birthed and built in Christ, on His Foundation, by His Foundation-Layers, in God's Timing – you may find yourself in a crowd gathered further than the eye can see (the "public" of "daily in public and from house to house"). You will likely be standing by someone you've never met (they gather in homes and apartment clubhouses on the south side of the city, and you on the northwest). And yet, there will be an immediate joy and camaraderie as you are both (obvious to each other by the depth and purity of spirit) Light-Walking! Confession of sin and bearing one another's burdens with a "total stranger" is the most natural thing in the (out-of-this-) world! It definitely won't be "two ships passing in the night" who happen to "attend services" together.

Watch and see!

Chapter Thirty-Two

"Conferences?"
"Concerts?"

N OW don't you dare read this chapter without reading all that precedes it – you will really miss my meaning if you don't understand the "why's" and the alternatives! But once again the key question is: "Is Jesus truly the Head, or not?"

Let's let Him be. No more "flesh on parade" with minimal accountability. That's how so many big-name traveling music and preaching folks have gotten into serious trouble. It is His CHURCH ("Ekklesia," "community") not talented or even dedicated individuals, that the gates of Hell cannot prevail against. It is His CHURCH ("community") that is the "Pillar and Foundation of Truth." It is His CHURCH that "makes known the manifold wisdom of God to the principalities and powers." "Christ in YOU (*plural*) – the Hope of GLORY!"

Instead of "concert" posters with mere men's names and faces advertised, and the horror of "autograph" signing, we had better consider returning to God's Way (as the Church returns to really being the Church)! A gift being expressed extra-locally should likely begin this way: the gifted one offers his life, his service as a "doulos" (a slave, a normal Christian), in the little practical things (Luke 16:10-12) to the church in his city of which he is a part. He becomes known as one "of good report;" he is emanating the Life of Jesus and bearing His Fruit. Through the course of normal life, that church invites the churches in other surrounding communities to gather with them at times. And if this tested "of good report" brother has gifts (music or otherwise) to share with the Body of Christ at large, he'll do that, just as the others do! If that gift is such that it would be an encouragement to the church in far-reaching lands, no doubt he will be sent out by the church (see Acts 13:1-4) along with other gifted men. There will be an accountability and brotherhood there that will challenge the pride and temptations that will eventually gain a foothold otherwise.

(Hebrews 3:12-13)

"See to it, brothers, that none of you has a sinful, unbelieving heart that turns away from the living God. But admonish (encourage, warn) one another daily, as long as it is called Today, so that none of you may be hardened by sin's deceitfulness."

The land is strewn with dead (or dying) men still singing songs and gathering crowds – though their lives are filled with pornography, materialism, temper, conceit and other unthinkable sin. (This is really happening amongst well-known musicians.) Christian music vendors around the world sing the same songs in the same order with the same intros, intermingling songs with the same rehashed touching stories and now-canned spiritual remarks . . . city after city.

I'm hopeful that not all are that way. And it usually didn't start out that way.

In the beginning, it was a man who wanted to express his gift to God and his brothers and sisters, and the "church" of which he was a part couldn't build or utilize that gift due to its improper foundation. He was forgotten or ridiculed or quenched. He was then encouraged by his friends to "give it a whirl" in the music industry; to have his own "ministry." (Can you imagine "Jesus of Nazareth Ministries" on the side of the fishing boat that Jesus crossed the Galilee in? Or a "radio ministry" introduced by the equivalent of, "Heeere's Jesus!" Or "Saul of Tarsus Ministries," with a neat logo, emblazoned on calling cards that Paul distributed?)

At one time, an honest, humble man offered to his Family the prayers and praises and encouragements that God had placed on his heart. But somehow, slowly, it had become a performance and a way to make a living. He wasn't a brother who would encourage in song anymore, but "a singing artist."

He used to say before singing a particular song:

"Please listen to the words of this song – you need to join me in this prayer to our Father!"

Now, in a not-necessarily-all-that-subtle expression of spiritual lethargy and "performance," before singing the same song, it's

"I wrote this song back before my hair was gray!" ("Audience" laughs.)

Hardness of heart and worldly conformity will set in, even in the most committed, when the "gift" they bear is not overflowing from the Life of the local church. It doesn't need to be this way! Erosion *will* occur when God's Ways are lost in the shuffle, or ignored, and the "ministry" becomes an independent entity that "uses" the local church or an advisory board as a figure-head substitute for daily accountability to God's People in His Church. A man, or woman, in such a disjointed, individualistic situation will often encounter much trauma as their marriages and children suffer needlessly. They will find themselves going to hear sermons in order to find inspiration for new songs, rather than to have their lives changed. All of this is unnecessarily tragic. There's a better way!

Instead of a "concert" in a city headlining a mere man, what if, as in the first century, a team of men with Ephesians 4:11 gifts were traveling from city to city as God directed. In the midst of those men was one with possibly a gift of music that was clearly (as with the others travelling with him with different gifts) to be a gift to the whole Body of Christ, rather than a "local Church" gift. All of those men, upon arriving in a city, offer their gifts in the context of the daily fabric of the local, visible church that is in that city.

Instead of the usual concert poster, in the context of Life that poster *could* read:

God's People, in the Power of the Holy Spirit, will likely

be gathering en masse at the Eagle Creek Pavilion next

Thursday evening after dinner.

As usual, we will together see how God leads us to

Celebrate His Goodness!

And some trustworthy gifted men of God from Nashville,

bearers of Light, Righteousness, Love, and Gifts from

Heaven in their various forms, will be joining us,

Lord willing.

Possibly God will use them in our midst as well.

Be sure and spread the word amongst the gatherings of

Believers of which you are a part between now and then,

and, of course, amongst the un-Believers you know

as well!

Oh, the integrity and security of such a thing! In our 20th-century worldly ways, if a "star" stayed up watching pornography and indulged his or her flesh in the hotel suite the night before a concert, who would know?[100]   And, (Thank you, P.T.) "The Show Must Go On!" What concerts do you know of (once the name has hit the charts) that have been canceled because the man or woman knew that he or she was out of fellowship with the Spirit and it would be hypocritical to pretend?

The momentum behind our worldly way to have religion and "ministry" is tremendous. "The auditorium is already rented!" "The television contract won't allow us to back out . . . we'd better just get our act together and go on." "But I have a contract with this publisher to write two more books in the next year . . . ."

These, and a myriad of other dilemmas, would never force us to run ahead of God (disobey Him) if we had not so mangled the church and the expression of gifts in the church. We have boldly intermixed worldly and music-vending showbiz principles with the Divine. That's not good! Let's bag the old and embrace God's Way – it's far better.

What about "Conferences?" Workshops, Lectureships, Seminars, Revival Meetings, Gospel Meetings . . . ? Is it possible for Believers from different cities to gather? Of course! The more the better!

Then how would something like that work?

You're probably assuming by now that it won't be a few "stars" chosen a year in advance, flown into town (often First Class), set up

---

[100] As in the televangelism circuit, it is common knowledge in the christian music "industry" that many powerful songs written and "performed" in the last decade have been written by those practicing immorality in various forms. Even the tape and CD covers of many of the most popular christian artists are embellished with photographs taken by a man referred to as (by the artists themselves) an occultic guru. Personally ask your favorite artist if he is not aware of, or even utilizing such ungodly men to promote their music. "Brothers, it ought not be so!" By His Grace, it can all be turned around!

at the Hyatt Regency, and asked to deliver a speech or two on some predetermined cleverly-titled subject. They then, to continue the far too accurate description of the norm, climb on their winged horses and gallop out of town, not to be seen again until the next extravaganza. (Meanwhile, who are they *really*? Is their life the "demonstration of the Spirit's Power?" You won't ever know. And if not, what does it matter what they *say*?) Could that be Jesus' way? Is that what Peter, John, Paul, and other men of God who *knew* Jesus did? Certainly not. And that is one strong reason why conference attenders by the thousands never really manifest the holiness, love, and power of God in their own lives, no matter how many conferences or workshops they pilgrimage to. Year after year spiritual poverty rampages their personal lives, families, and churches. Why?

What is wrong with the mode of religious activities today that includes christian "experts," "stars," and "special guest speakers and performers?" This is a little hard to express, but bear with me for a moment. *God never promised to transform lives through things that are projected from a stage to an "audience."* Jesus, the Rosetta Stone, the Translation Key of the Father's Heart, wasn't like that.

God's way to transform lives is this:

(2Corinthians 4:7)
*"But we have this treasure in **earthen** vessels, that the excellence of the power may be of God and not of us."*

(2Corinthians 3:3)
*"**You** are manifestly an epistle of Christ, ministered by us, written not with ink but by the Spirit of the living God, not on tablets of stone but on tablets of flesh, that is, of **the heart**."*

(1Thessalonians 2:7-13)
*"But we [Paul, Silas, Timothy] were gentle among you, just as a nursing mother cherishes her own children. So, affectionately longing for you, we were well pleased to impart to you not only the gospel of God, but also **our own lives**, because you had become dear to us. For you remember, brethren, our labor and toil; for laboring night and day, that we might not be a burden to any of you, we heralded to you the gospel of God. You are witnesses, and God also, how devoutly and justly*

and blamelessly we behaved ourselves among you who believe; as you
know how we exhorted, and comforted, and charged every one of you,
as a father does his own children, that you would have a walk worthy
of God who calls you into His own kingdom and glory. For this reason
we also thank God without ceasing, because when you received the word
of God which you heard from us, you welcomed it not as the word of
men, but as it is in truth, the word of God, which also effectively works
in you who believe."

The Good News of Jesus and His Body on earth was, and is, brought in the context of LIFE, not in speeches or performances. Paul likened himself to a mother, a brother, and a father. Did *your* mother set the family in rows and columns and deliver speeches to you? Families aren't grown up in a classroom test tube. They walk together. "Consider that field over there . . . ."

That's how our Lord lived with them . . . and changed them. "It is the same now."

(Luke 22:27)
"For who is greater, he who sits at the table, or he who serves?
Is it not he who sits at the table? Yet I am among you as the One who
serves."

(Mark 3:14)
"Then He appointed twelve, that they might be with Him and
that He might send them out."

(John 1:4, 14)
"The Life became the Light of men . . . And the Word became
flesh and dwelt among us, and we beheld His glory."

The gifts of God aren't delivered from behind a pulpit or from a stage. They are "in our midst." Their "lives" bring the Light. They express themselves "among us" – not as traveling speech-givers and heroes of profundity.

So what are the alternatives? How can we tap the gifts in the Body of Christ on a multi-city level? Again, my desire is to provoke you to pursue the Head, Jesus Himself – not to run after gimmicks, new or old. For that reason, and because I'm still learning myself, I'm not going to give you much. But here's a thought to carefully pray about, as a seed for the future, when God does pour forth His Light and Splendor:

Dear Saints. Some tested, fruitful men

will be in our city for however long God directs.

These men have kicked in satan's teeth in cities

all over the globe.

Spread the word amongst the different gatherings you

are in through the next week that the whole church will

be together daily (for as much as you can get there for),

beginning next Thursday . . . for who knows how long!

No doubt many of you will see the

manifestations of Godliness in the

highways and byways and from house to house

as these men are in our midst to show us

God's Love and washbasin. Seek "equipping"

(Eph.4:11-17)!

The "Dome" is reserved for us,

beginning at eight in the morning each day.

Come having considered how **you** might

"spur one another on to love and good works."

Bring your gifts to the streets and the gatherings,

and these brothers, as God directs,

will bring theirs.

Let's celebrate Jesus together and see what happens!

Chapter Thirty-Three

A Request

BEFORE GOD, MY FRIENDS, as far as my feeble heart can do such a Godly thing, I love you. This book is in no way intended to be insulting. God has been very, very merciful to me in spite of the foolishness and sin that I have given myself over to, at times, in rebellion to my Lord. I don't, and can not, make any claims for myself. I stand only by the same unmerited favor by which He saved me in the first place. And so, I ask your forgiveness if I have hurt anyone or have been the catalyst of any foolish reactionism in immature disciples. I have no glee in having spoken so frankly.

"I tell the truth in Christ, I am not lying, my conscience also bearing me witness in the Holy Spirit, that I have great sorrow and continual grief in my heart. For I could wish that I myself were accursed from Christ for my brethren . . . "

If you've been enraged by and are indignant at the thoughts contained in this book because you've read it with a darkened heart, intentionally trying to find items that you can take exception to, that's not good. If you've read dishonestly that you might attempt to "prove" otherwise – to save your clergy job or lazy lifestyle, or to protect the memory of "good ole Grandpa Clevis, the churchman," then there is nothing that I can say to you. Except "may God have mercy on you (and all of us), and may He protect others from your influence as long as you are such."

But if you are just thoroughly confused because of my poor communication skills, or bordering on despair since the answers to "What should I do next?" are not obvious right now, then I want you to know that it's okay. You can be frustrated with me, or angry, and I don't blame you at all.[101] I dumped a truckload on you all at

---

[101] However, just a thought about a subject that few have considered, since books seem to be such impersonal things. Remember for others' sake, and your own, that people who write books are sometimes your brothers and sisters. Don't treat them as a faceless name that expresses ideas. For Jesus' sake, treat them and the

once. Had I been with you, I would have walked you into higher ground rather than just pointing at the fruitless, withered fig tree and *telling* you of a Higher way. Nevertheless, if you purposely forget all that you have just read and continue on your way, please, at least, don't ever settle for less than what our Father desires for you personally, your family, and the church of which you are a part. Ever? Okay?

(Hebrews 11:9-16, applied)
"By faith your heart has made its home in the Promised Land of God's Truth like a stranger in a foreign country. You live, for now, in tents (a total contradiction of what your heart has longed for), as do so many fellow heirs of the same promise. For you are looking forward to the City with Foundations, whose Builder and Maker is God Himself.

"Though all the facts, and all of your personal history may scream out that it's too late, you're barren and it can't be done – you will be enabled to bear fruit from Heaven, because you continue to consider Him faithful Who has made the Promise. And so from mere men like yourself, men as good as dead, will come descendants as numerous as the stars in the sky and as countless as the sand on the seashore.

"And all these people will live by faith, if even until death. If they do not receive the things promised, they only see them and welcome them from a distance – they will press on. And they will admit that they are aliens and strangers on this planet.

"People who say such things show that they themselves are looking relentlessly for the Kingdom of our Lord, the expression of His Reign in His People. If they had been thinking of the worldly pleasures, security, and the religion of this age that they had left, they would have had opportunity to return. Instead, they are longing for a better country – one clearly "Born of God," a Church that the gates of Hell can no longer prevail against. Therefore God is not ashamed to be called their God, for he has prepared a City for them."

---

words that they have risked to offer to you with the respect that Christ has called us to offer one another. They may never know what you've said, and that really is not important anyway, but keep your record clean with the Holy Spirit whenever you speak of another. For the Testimony of Jesus.

Hang tough, pilgrims![102]   As our brother Isaiah has said, "God does not bring to the point of birth, and not give delivery!" As we pray the prayer that Jesus called out to His Father, "Father! Glorify your Name!" we can joyfully and expectantly await a similar answer from our Father, "I have glorified it. And I'll glorify it again!"

In keeping with that heart, please remember that none of this was written that a new generation of fault-finders, revolutionaries,

---

[102] The pouring out of God's Glory in an unmistakable way is a very Sovereign thing. Though faithfulness and absolute obedience to Jesus is the only choice we would ever desire as followers of His, all of the faithfulness in the world cannot make God blow the whole show wide open as He did in the first century. When God is "shaking everything that can be shaken," a simple fisherman's rebuttal to an accusation that he had a drinking problem results in three thousand conversions in a matter of hours (Acts 2:1-47). Handkerchiefs and mere men's shadows become instruments of devastation to the enemy's strongholds (Acts 5:15, 19:11-12). That kind of manifestation of Power is God's Sovereign choice.

The good news is this: God has fulfilled two of the three Jewish Feasts, Passover and Pentecost, in a profound and very visible way. There is much reason from Scripture to anticipate that the final and greatest of the three Feasts, Tabernacles, will be every bit as profound and visible. (See The Church Alive if this is of interest to you.) Expect another season of awesome Glory. Prepare the way.

Until that time, as one brother has said, don't be bought, compromised, detoured, delayed, or deluded. Don't flinch in the face of adversity, negotiate at the table of the enemy, or meander in the maze of mediocrity.

Though the victories, apart from God's outpouring, will be much more demanding, carry on - basing the convictions of your heart on Truth alone. Be relentless and Faithful in carrying on God's Work. Regardless of results, press on. No matter how few your companions, stand in the gap. Though you may feel as if you are trying to bail out the Titanic "a thimbleful at a time," bail on! For Jesus' sake.

History has known times of little Glory. Even Paul encountered some of this in his last days when he was rejected by "everyone in the province of Asia" - not long after he had spent three years warning them "night and day, in tears." Yet we press faithfully on, with our hands to the plow and no rear-view mirrors.

In times of little Sovereign Glory, we'll fight the enemy for men's souls in hand-to-hand combat, with short daggers. But, oh, for the return of the days where God equips us with hand grenades. Then, like Jesus, and as in the early days of the Church, we can blow up the enemy - and we don't even have to be there! Multi-thousands can be instantly brought to a maturity level that doesn't piddle around with foolishness, but, on day one, "all the believers are together and have all things in common," fully "devoted to the apostles' teaching, to the fellowship, to the breaking of bread, and to prayer." God did that once already (Acts 2:38-47; 4:32-35; Ezek.36:26-27, 37:1-10). Is the Arm of the Lord too short? Prepare your life and heart for Tabernacles! Make straight paths for the Coming of the Lord.

and "experts" in "how to have church" might arise. It was written to give a Vision and Hope to God's true-hearted People. It was written to "divide between soul and Spirit" . . . to expose motives, contend with the flesh that lingers in each of us, and to allow the folly of Jannes and Jambres, Korah, Ichabod, Nicholas, and Diotrephes to be "evident to all."

And it is essential that I say goodbye to you by reminding you that our battle is not with ideas and formats.

(Ephesians 6:12)
"For our struggle is not against flesh and blood, but against the rulers, against the authorities, against the powers of this dark world and against the spiritual forces of evil in the heavenly realms."

And that being the case, the only place Victory over those principalities and powers can be attained . . . is at the Cross.

(Colossians 2:15)
"And having disarmed the powers and authorities, he made a public spectacle of them, triumphing over them by the cross."

Our course is secure because it is cemented in a tenacious, bold, peace-filled, night-and-day Hope . . . made sure by the Blood of Christ. No matter what else happens! And a cross that you pick up for others, "while they're yet sinners."

There will be no Victory based on good ideas; only on your cross for others and by your total Trust in Jesus and His Atonement will Satan be made a spectacle and publicly humiliated.

You'll know who cares, who is genuine in their desire to follow Jesus, but is just needing help. Stand by those guys. And you'll know who the charlatans are by whom you must not allow yourself to be shackled and blackmailed. **Judge for yourselves whether its better to obey God or men.**

Towards those who truly desire to follow our Lord Jesus, offer your unlimited love as you work out the preceding Truths. And we'll see y'all at Home sometime soon.

(Romans 15:1-7)

"We who are strong ought to bear with the failings of the weak and not to please ourselves. Each of us should please his neighbor for his good, to build him up. For even Christ did not please Himself but, as it is written: 'The insults of those who insult you have fallen on me.' For everything that was written in the past was written to teach us, so that through endurance and the encouragement of the Scriptures we might have Hope.

"May the God Who gives endurance and encouragement grant you to be like minded toward one another, as you follow Christ Jesus, so that with one mind and one mouth you may glorify the God and Father of our Lord Jesus Christ.

"Therefore receive one another, just as Christ also received us, to the Glory of God."

Together

Gather for and with our Jesus,
Tell Him that you love Him.
Sing to Him with all your heart
That you'll have no one above Him.

Bare your heart – it's the only way
To come near to Him and others.
Renounce your fears, your pride, the world
To share true Life with Brothers.

Meet the needs that run oh, so deep.
Declare His Truths, you Priests of God!
Gather mightily in His Name:
Hear His Voice, Eat His Bread, Learn His Rod.

Do not fret, His Little Ones,
When times seem hard and His Work, no end.
He knows we're His Toddlers, just giving our all
And with His gladness undaunted He'll continue to Send.

From every Nation, tongue, and tribe
God's Family will stand as One:
Loving and Living, Reproving and Giving
Until the Battle's won.

Gather with Jesus;
Sing loud and hug soft.
Celebrate with your Family –
Join with them oft.

Mike

I AM Here

I'll be with you in the sunny hours,
I'll be with you in the rain,
I'll be with you when your heart is joyful
and when you're full of pain.
You say the road's too rough for you,
You say it's far too long,
But I AM there to take your hand
And I will make you strong.

Because I AM your Father.
And I AM your friend.
And I want you to be like me,
I'll carry you to the end.

Cindy

I recognize that "Family" and "Army" are not
synonyms for "church" in the experience of most.
Self-sacrifice, vulnerability, courage, and holiness,
presented to you now in this writing as a way of Life
for every church of Jesus,
have probably not been a huge part
of your church experience as you have grown up . . . .
They need to be - from here on Home.
Even the "angels long to look into these things."
The demons are awestruck and trembling
at the infinite Wisdom of our God.[a]

How could God possibly use mere humans such as you and me
to publicly humiliate the principalities and rulers of wickedness
in this life,
and to bring about their final defeat?!
The demons loathe the fact that **THERE's a MAN**[b] **in heaven!**
And, worse yet for these repulsive foes of God and our Faith,
this Man of men is **only the first of a whole new Race!**
Not only will our God obliterate the hateful uprising of satan
and his disciples,
but He will even use, as He Revealed in His "Firstborn,"
mere mortal men, washed in the Blood of the Lamb
and learning to walk in His Spirit, to do it.
Though He has created us "a little *lower* than the angels,"
He will *build* us, in His Church
(in the measure that we are willing to bear His Cross for others),
into His Stature and Character and Fullness as His Habitation.[c]
It is a concluded matter that our God will, in this way,
bring about the public shellacking of the enemy!
So be it. Maranatha.

---

[a] Ephesians 3:10, 6:12; 1Peter 1:12-13; Colossians 2:15, 1:15-20.

[b] Acts 7:55-56; Hebrews 2:14-18, 4:14-5:8; Philippians 2:6-8; 2John 7.

[c] Ephesians 2:22; 1Peter 2:4-12; 1John 3:1-10, 5:18-21, 2:8-14; Romans 16:20; Matthew 16:16-18.